Creating A Legend

Commander Tyrone G. Martin
U. S. Navy (Retired)

Illustrations by
John Charles Roach
U.S. Navy Combat Artist
&
Samuel F. Manning

A Timonier Book

TRYON PUBLISHING COMPANY, INC.
CHAPEL HILL • TRYON

Also by the author

UNDEFEATED: OLD IRONSIDES IN THE WAR OF 1812
A MOST FORTURNATE SHIP

Copyright © 1997 Tyrone G. Martin
All rights reserved. No part of this book may be reproduced
in any form or by any electronic, mechanical or other means,
except for brief quotes for reviews, without express written
permission from the publisher.

Published by
Tryon Publishing Company, Inc.
P.O. Box 1138
Chapel Hill, North Carolina
Printed in the United States of America
by MA Designs

Cover & Book Design by Julia Calhoun Williams

First Edition
First Printing

ISBN 1-884824-20-X

TABLE OF CONTENTS

Introduction   *v*

PART I -   *THE NEED FOR A NAVY*   11
PART II -   *THE DESIGNER AND HIS DESIGN*   21
PART III -   *THE BUILDING TEAM AND CONTRACTS*   43
PART IV -   *BUILDING THE SHIP*   55
PART V -   *THE LAUNCH*   77
PART VI -   *COMPLETION AND COST*   89

Afterword   *103*

Appendix A -   Table of Dimensions of a Frigate of 44 Guns   105
Appendix B -   Joshua Humphreys' Material Estimate for a 44-gun Frigate   115
Appendix C -   Specifications for *Constitution*'s Original 24-Pounder Guns   118
Appendix D -   Standing Rigging for Frigate *Constitution* 1797   119

Bibliography   121

ILLUSTRATIONS

The Eagle Crest Worn by CONSTITUTION	11
Ship's Boat - Wherry	21
Builder's Draught for Frigate CONSTITUTION	26
Diagram of Diagonal Supports	28
Birth (Berth) Deck	29
Gun Deck	30
Upper Deck	31
Structural Detail	35
Ship's Anchor	43
Building the Ship	55
Cutting the Timbers	57, 58
Structural Detail	60
Ship Building in Progress	64, 65
Structural Section	69
Blocks & Lines	77
The Launching of the Constitution	81
Ship's Wheel	89
Transparent View of Bow	91
Transparent View of Stern	94
Gun Deck & Anchor Detail	97
Rigging out the Studding Sails	99

INTRODUCTION

USS Constitution is one of the most well known ships in the world, along with British Admiral Horatio Nelson's *HMS Victory* and Japanese Admiral Heihachiro Togo's *HIJMS Mikasa*. But, as *Victory* is revered as Nelson's flagship at the Battle of Trafalgar in 1805 and *Mikasa* as Togo's at the Battle of Tsushima a century later, *Constitution* is remembered and honored as an undefeated champion, victor in a series of battles fought at different times and involving different commanders. In that sense, she has a more universal heritage. Given her string of victories, then, one would logically assume that there was something more than the skill of her several captains on those occasions that contributed to her success — something involving the physical characteristics of the ship.

This volume attempts to provide clues in that regard. It recalls the designer's enlightened philosophy as to what our infant Navy needed in the way of fighting ships. And it delineates the designer's genius in devising an innovative structure that would result in her nickname – "Old Ironsides," and contribute significantly to her continued existence today. This is also the story of her construction, launching, and outfitting – and the events leading to that moment when she first went to sea, beginning a career that continues today. "Old Ironsides'" grand tradition includes being the oldest commissioned warship afloat in the world.

The author is indebted to Navy Combat Artist and friend John Charles Roach, whose evocative sketches have rendered technical details comprehensible. His illustrations of Joshua Humphreys' innovative structural ideas originally appeared in *Naval History* magazine.

A debt, too, is owed Virginia Steele Wood, research specialist and naval reader at the Library of Congress, for her unstinting efforts in answering the author's queries regarding the central participants in this historical account.

My thanks to the USS Constitution Museum and to Samuel F. Manning for permission to use several of his sketches in the book.

Charles Deems, Donald A. Turner, and Patrick Otton of the Naval Historical Center Detachment, Boston, were most generous with their time in sharing their research and reviewing the structural details on site aboard *Constitution*.

Tyrone G. Martin
Devil's Ridge 1 April 1996

Creating A Legend

Part I
The Need for a Navy

The long, exhausting Revolution was over. The American Confederation was independent. Fighting was done. Enemies, officially at least, were friends. Nonetheless, there were those in the Congress who hoped to maintain a semblance of a navy as a symbol of national honor and as a deterrent to those who would interfere with American trade on the high seas. It was soon seen, however, that the maintenance of even a single frigate was more than the penniless nation could afford. The last unit of the Continental Navy was sold in August 1785.

The few who attempted to maintain a navy were aware that the Barbary pirates of North Africa had pounced with delight on the merchantmen of the new nation as soon as they appeared in the Mediterranean. In their last years as colonials, Americans annually sent eighty to a hundred ships, carrying some 1200 seamen, to the Middle Sea in this trade – under the protection of the Royal Navy. The Revolution ended that protection.

The American experience with the raiders began very soon after the colonies were established. In 1625, two Pilgrim ships were captured and taken into Sale, Morocco. New York merchant Jacob Leiser and ten others were captured by Algerines in 1678 and held for a large ransom, which was raised by the churches of New York City.

Within the week of the end of the Continental Navy, there occurred two seizures of interest to our story in the Mediterranean. The first was the schooner *Maria*, out of Boston, by a 14-gun Algerine xebec. One of the captives was James Leander Cathcart, who would play an influential role in the Barbary Wars two decades later. The second was the ship *Dauphin* of Philadelphia, whose captain, Richard O'Brien, also would serve a diplomatic role in solving the pirate problem. Shocking and outrageous as these acts were, they stirred no national commotion in the United States. In 1786, Congress designated Benjamin Franklin, head of the American commissioners in France, Thomas Jefferson, soon to be Minister to France, and John Adams, soon to be our Minister at the Court of St. James, to seek the release of the *Marie* and *Dauphin* crews.

The Americans sent an agent to the Algerine Dey to learn of his demands. He reported the asking price was $56,496, or about $2850 a head. This clearly exorbitant claim was rejected by Jefferson, who, although without Congressional authority, responded through an intermediary with an offer of $200 per man. This was rejected by the Dey and negotiations languished, as did the Americans in slavery. Franklin soon returned to Philadelphia. Jefferson likewise returned to Philadelphia in 1789 to the post of Secretary of State in the new Constitutional government.

A year later, Jefferson forwarded to President Washington a study he had completed on the Barbary problem. He suggested there were three options: (1) insure cargoes, ransom prisoners regularly at a fixed rate, and conduct commerce as usual; (2) buy safe conduct with tribute, as many European nations did; or (3) fight. The Congress also studied this report, and decided that ransom would cost less than creating a navy.

Congress finally appropriated the necessary monies in May 1792. Jefferson dispatched our new Minister to London, Thomas Pinckney, with instructions to stop in Paris enroute and deliver to John Paul Jones, then residing there, the President's appointment as negotiator. The plan died a-borning as Jones was dead by the time Pinckney got to Paris, and the alternate, Thomas Barclay in Lisbon, died just after the instructions reached him.

There now occurred an event, involving no Americans, which ultimately would bring about the establishment of the United States Navy and deliver relief to the long-suffering captives. Charles Logis, British Consul in Algiers, working independently behind the scenes, concluded a truce in the seven-year war between Algiers and Portugal. This resulted in the cessation of Portuguese naval activities in the Strait of Gibraltar, where they had been the "cork in the bottle," holding the pirates in the Middle Sea. Soon, the corsairs were active in the Atlantic. The final three months of 1793 gave Americans a jolt:

eleven merchantmen were taken by pirates and more than one hundred crewmen were held for ransom.

The Algerine rapacity that spurred the Third Congress into action marked the beginning of the successful legislative effort to create a navy, but not the first effort. In 1789, immediately after the House of Representatives was organized, James Madison introduced a revenue bill which considered, in part, the collection of revenue that would be used to strengthen the country's maritime defenses. In 1790, such considerations led to the creation of the Revenue Marine, precursor to the modern Coast Guard. And in November 1791, Secretary of War Knox submitted several estimates concerning the maintenance costs of different types of warships to a Senate committee.[1] None of these actions resulted in any positive moves toward a navy.

The Third Congress convened on 2 December 1793, and soon was concerned with the irksome problems of continued Indian troubles on the frontier, as well as the rather cavalier treatment of neutral shipping by Anglo-French belligerents. The newspapers of Philadelphia carried the first stunning accounts of the Algerine depredations in the Atlantic on 8 December. President Washington sent Congress a message on the subject on the 16th, accompanied by a State Department report on foreign trade. In the weeks to follow, secret debates were conducted in the House against a background of fact and fiction appearing in the local press. It adopted by a narrow margin three resolutions on 2 January 1794 to (1) appropriate additional money for diplomatic expenses; (2) provide a naval force sufficient to protect American commerce from the Algerine corsairs; and (3) establish a committee to determine the size and cost of this force.

The Select Committee, composed of six Federalists and three Republicans, was heavy with pro-shipping people. Its report, delivered on 20 January, was based upon the estimates Secretary Knox had accumulated in previous years, in addition to those documents most recently provided by the President and the Secretary of State. The Committee recommended that four 44-gun (armed with 18- and 9-pounder long guns) and two 20-gun ships be constructed for the optimistically small sum of $600,000.

The House debate on this report began on 16 February and split along predictable North-South, inland-tidewater lines. Opponents argued that the proposed naval force was too expensive, was a menace to democratic government, was inadequate, and that its development could both upset the British and render negotiations with the Algerines more difficult. The pro-navy people responded that, while expensive in itself, this naval force would cost less than the inflated insurance rates being paid by the merchant marine, and that a defenseless government was equally in danger of being overthrown. Furthermore, the proponents argued that the proposed force was adequate for the intended limited purpose, and for this reason, too, would be less of a burden than a full-blown navy and less of a menace to civil liberties. In sum, they were saying that the force would be too weak to do more than overpower the pirates.

The debate was a month old when Washington sent over additional supporting documents. Among these was a 27 November 1793 letter from Consul David Humphries in Lisbon, in which he stated "a naval force has now (to a certain degree) become indispensable," and another from Richard O'Brien, now in his ninth year of captivity, who had changed his mind about the use of force and said there was "no alternative." Additional help for the proponents came on 5 March in the form of a petition from Baltimore merchants for an adequate naval force. And final impetus came just two days later when the news of the British Orders in Council prohibiting all neutral trade in the French West Indies outraged the Congressmen.

The complete bill was brought to a vote in the House on 10 March. It was passed 50-39. The opposition had been further weakened by a provision requiring the termination of construction should a peace treaty with Algiers be signed. Senate action seems never to have been in doubt, and on 19 March the bill was approved without division. President Washington signed "An act to provide a naval armament" on 27 March 1794. It read:

> "Whereas the depredations committed by the Algerine corsairs on the commerce of the United States render it necessary that a naval force should be provided for its protection:
>
> "SECTION 1. Be it therefore enacted by the Senate and House of Representatives of the United States of America in Congress assembled, that the President of the United States be authorized to provide, by purchase or otherwise, equip and employ four ships to carry forty-four guns each, and two ships to carry thirty-six guns each.
>
> "SECTION 2. And be it further enacted, that there shall be employed on board each of the ships of forty-four guns, one captain, four lieutenants, one lieutenant of marines, one chaplain, one surgeon, and two surgeon's mates; and in each of the ships of thirty-six guns, one captain, three lieutenants, and one lieutenant of marines, one surgeon, and one

surgeon's mate, who shall be appointed and commissioned in like manner as other officers of the United States are.

"SECTION 3. And be it further enacted, that there shall be employed, in each of said ships, the following warrant officers, who shall be appointed by the President of the United States, to wit: One sailing master, one purser, one boatswain, one gunner, one sail-maker, one carpenter, and eight midshipmen; and the following petty officers, who shall be appointed by the captains of the ships, respectively, in which they shall be employed, viz.; two master's mates, one captain's clerk, two boatswain's mates, one cockswain, one sail-maker's mate, two gunner's mates, one yeoman of the gunroom, nine quarter-gunners (and for the four larger ships two additional quarter-gunners), two carpenter's mates, one armourer, one steward, one cooper, one master-at-arms, and one cook.

"SECTION 4. And be it further enacted, that the crews of each of the said ships of forty-four guns, shall consist of one hundred and fifty seamen, one hundred and three midshipmen and ordinary seamen, one sergeant, one corporal, one drum, one fife, and fifty marines; and that the crews of each of the said ships of thirty-six guns shall consist of one hundred and thirty able seamen and midshipmen, ninety ordinary seamen, one sergeant, two corporals, one drum, one fife, and forty marines, over and above the officers herein before mentioned.

"SECTION 5. And be it further enacted, that the President of the United States be, and he is further empowered, to provide, by purchase or otherwise, in lieu of the said six ships, a naval force not exceeding, in the whole, that by this act directed, so that no ships thus provided shall carry less than thirty-two guns; or he may so provide any proportion thereof, which, in his discretion, he may think proper.

"SECTION 6. And be it further enacted, that the pay and subsistence of the respective commissioned and warrant officers be as follows: A captain, seventy-five dollars per month, and six rations per day; a lieutenant, forty dollars per month, and three rations per day; a lieutenant of marines, twenty-six dollars per month, and two rations per day; a chaplain, forty dollars per month, and two rations per day; a sailing-master, forty dollars per month, and two rations per day; a surgeon, fifty dollars per month, and two rations per day; a surgeon's mate, thirty dollars per month, and two rations per day; a purser, forty dollars per month, and two rations per day; a boatswain, fourteen dollars per month, and two rations per day; a gunner, fourteen dollars per month, and two rations per day; a sailmaker, fourteen dollars per month, and two rations per day; a carpenter, fourteen dollars per month, and two rations per day.

"SECTION 7. And be it further enacted, that the pay to be allowed to the petty officers, midshipmen, seamen, ordinary seamen, and marines shall be fixed by the President of the United States: Provided, that the whole sum to be given for the whole pay aforesaid, shall not exceed twenty seven thousand dollars per month, and that each of the said persons shall be entitled to one ration per day.

"SECTION 8. And be it further enacted, that the ration shall consist of, as follows: Sunday one pound of bread, one pound and a half of beef, and one pound of rice: Monday, one pound of bread, one pound of pork, half a pint of peas or beans, and four ounces of cheese: Tuesday, one pound of bread, one pound and a half of beef, and one pound of pota toes or turnips, and pudding: Wednesday, one pound of bread, two ounces of butter, or in lieu thereof, six ounces of molasses, four ounces of cheese, and a half pint of rice: Thursday, one pound of bread, one pound of pork, and a half pint of peas or beans: Friday, one pound of bread, one pound of salt fish, two ounces of butter, or one gill of oil, and one pound of potatoes: Saturday, one pound of bread, one pound of pork, half a pint of peas or beans, and four ounces of cheese: And there shall also be allowed one half pint of distilled spirits per day, or, in lieu thereof, one quart of beer per day, to each ration.

"SECTION 9. Provided always, and be it further enacted, that if a peace shall take place between the United States and the Regency of Algiers, that no further proceedings be had under this act."

Such was the legislative germ of the United States Navy.

NOTE:

1. There being no Secretary of the Army or of the Navy, the first Secretary of War was analogous to today's "Secretary of Defense."

Part II
The Designer & His Design

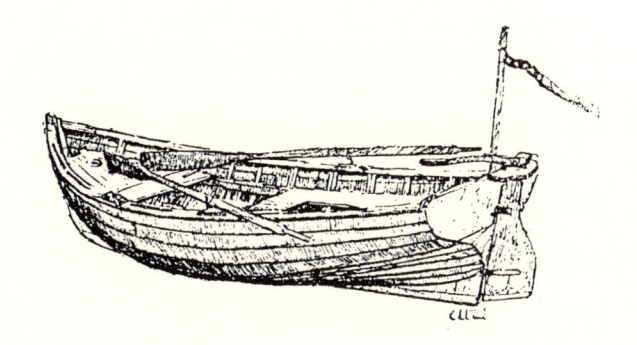

The few signposts extant indicate that Secretary of War Henry Knox had been studying the problem of beginning a naval force for some time before President Washington signed the enabling legislation. He was corresponding with naval veterans of the Revolution within a year after the establishment of the Federal Government. One of those contacted was John Foster Williams, one-time captain of the Massachusetts state frigate *Protector*. On 30 October 1790, he wrote to Knox:

> "Agreeably to your request, I enclose an estimate of a frigate of nine hundred tons, and believe it to be not far wide of what will be the real cost, but as the circumstances would not admit of my being too open in my enquiries, it may vary a little. The cost of the guns and warlike stores you can form a better judgment of than myself. The timber, &c., should be cut in the fall of the year, as that would add much to its duration. Should any further inquiries be necessary, or any services that I can render be acceptable, shall be happy in being favored with your commands."

Others consulted by Knox were James Hackett of Portsmouth, New Hampshire, builder of the Continental Navy's *Alliance*, considered by many to have been the finest American frigate of the day; Captain John Barry, who had commanded both *Alliance* and the brig

Lexington during the Revolution; and John Wharton, a shipbuilder of Philadelphia whose firm had built the Continental frigate *Randolph*. The following letter to Senator Robert Morris, from Joshua Humphreys, Wharton's cousin and one-time business partner, is further evidence of the tight little group in consultation with Secretary Knox and, in light of later developments, is a good summation of the consensus of their advice. It is dated 6 January 1793, but the opening statement seems to indicate that Humphreys meant to date it "1794:"

> "From the present appearance of affairs I believe it is time this country was possessed of a Navy; but as that is yet to be raised I have ventured a few ideas on that subject.
>
> "Ships that compose the European navys [sic] are generally distinguished by their rates; but as the situation and depth of water of our coast and harbors are different in some degrees from those in Europe, and as our navy must for a considerable time be inferior in numbers, we are to consider what size ships will be most formidable and be an over match for those of an enemy; such Frigates as in blowing weather would be an overmatch for double deck ships, and in light winds to evade coming to action, or double deck ships as would be an over match for common double deck ships and in blowing weather superior to ships of three decks, or in calm weather or light winds to outsail them. Ships built on these principles will render those of an enemy in a degree useless, or require a greater number before they dare attack our ship. Frigates, I suppose, will be the first object and none ought to be built less than 150 feet keel to carry 28 32-pounders or 30 24-pounders on the gun deck and 12-pounders on the quarterdeck. These ships should have scantlings equal to 74's, and I believe may be built of red cedar and live oak for about twenty-four pounds per ton, carpenters tonnage including carpenters bill, smiths including anchors, joiners, boat-builders, painters, plumbers, carvers, coopers, block makers, mast makers, riggers and rigging, sail makers and sail cloth, suits and chandlers bill. As such ships will cost a large sum of money they should be built of the best materials that could possibly be procured, the beams of their decks should be of the best Carolina pine, and the lower futtocks and knees if possible of Live Oak.
>
> "The greatest care should be taken in the construction of such ships, and particularly all her timbers should be framed and bolted together before they are raised. Frigates built to

carry 12 and 18-pounders in my opinion will not answer the expectation contemplated from them, for if we should be obliged to take part in the present European war, or at a future day we should be dragged into a war with any powers of the Old Continent, especially Great Britain, they having such a number of ships of that size, that it would be an equal chance by equal combat that we lose our ships and more particularly from the Algerians who have ships and some of greater force. Several questions will arise whether one large or two small frigates contribute most to the protection of our trade or which will cost the least sum of money, or whether two small ones are as able to engage a double deck ship as one large one. For my part I am decidedly of the opinion the large ones will answer best."

Who was Joshua Humphreys and how did he come to be selected as the designer of the authorized frigates? He was born in Haverford, Pennsylvania, on 17 June 1751, the son of Welsh Quakers who first arrived in the colonies in 1682. At the age of about 14, he was apprenticed to James Penrose, a well-known Philadelphia shipwright and builder. When Penrose died in 1771, shortly before Humphreys completed his apprenticeship, the Widow Penrose remitted his time and hired him as master shipwright to complete a vessel then building at her late husband's yard.

In 1774, Joshua, now 23, went into partnership with his older cousin, John Wharton. Wharton was a close friend of Robert Morris, a politician close to both Continental and provincial shipbuilding. It was the firm of Wharton and Humphreys that built the frigate *Randolph* (32 guns), which was launched in 1776. The design, on which Humphreys may have worked, was of a sharp frigate of conventional layout in the British pattern, but larger than the standard for the rate. The hull form, too, differed from contemporary British or French designs in that it had much more deadrise in the bottom, rounder curves in cross section, far more rake to the bow, and a little more depth and freeboard. Perhaps surprising in view of later efforts by Humphreys, the framing was lighter than in similar British units. Clearly, the design reflected elements found in both contemporary French and British construction, but these were combined with peculiarly American requirements, e. g., a greater emphasis on speed.

Whatever his role as a ship designer and builder during the Revolution, in the years following the war's end Humphreys became an established shipbuilder in Philadelphia. The reason he had access to the Secretary of War undoubtedly was due more to his connections and his residence in Philadelphia than to any preeminence in his chosen field. Too, it is evident from the letter quoted earlier, and in other correspondence, that he was interested in the subject and had given it serious attention on his own initiative.

Designing a ship is somewhat like doing your income tax: you must manipulate a great number of values in such a way that they present a unified result reasonably satisfactory to all concerned. The first consideration is the purpose to which the ship will be put: merchantman or man-of-war? For cargo? To be in the battle line? To do what? Having decided that, the marine architect must then decide which characteristics are to be emphasized: Speed? Carrying capacity? Weaponry? Endurance? Then, he must think about how many will be required in the crew; how much food, fuel, and ammunition will be carried; and many, many other things that will result in the creation of a mobile, floating, largely self-sustaining community fulfilling some useful purpose.

When Congress authorized the construction of the first warships for the United States Navy, it already had made a major decision for the naval architect when it decreed that the ships would be frigates, the middle size of warship in those days, like cruisers in the modern Navy. By definition, a frigate was a warship with one covered gun deck which might also carry some guns above on its open "weather" deck.

Humphreys first undertook to make a half model of his proposed hull design so that both politicians and other shipbuilders could see what he intended and offer suggestions. This he did as the result of a request from Secretary Knox on 12 April, well before his formal appointment as Naval Constructor, dated 28 June 1794. In accordance with his earlier letter, he proposed a frigate rated to carry 44 long guns on a hull some 175 feet long at the waterline and more than 44 feet wide. The resultant ship would be both longer and wider than most English or French counterparts, with over fifteen percent more guns of larger caliber. It would be a "heavy frigate," the battle cruiser of her day.

Humphreys had to come up with a hull form that would be stable, when fully loaded, under most conditions of wind and weather. It had to be of adequate volume to be able to carry her guns, shot and powder, as well as the sails and rigging to provide her with adequate propulsion, the men to operate the guns and handle the rigging, and the food, water, and supplies to permit operations independent of the shore for an extended period of time. Except for water, the ship should be able to operate for six months without recourse to outside assistance. The ship also had to have reasonably good speed to meet the designer's own criteria of being able to outmaneuver an opponent or get out of the way of one stronger. And it had to have sturdy construction to withstand storms and enemy gunfire (the "scantlings of a 74"). What he had to come up with was a fast, powerful ship with heavy armament and the capability to operate independently just about anywhere in the world.

Unlike today, when the plans for a warship will run to thousands of sheets, those for *Constitution* appeared on but a single sheet. On it were three views of the ship.

The uppermost one was the sheer plan, the side view or profile of the ship. It showed the longitudinal curve ("sheer") of the ship and the curve of the decks to match it. It also showed the length and depth of the keel, the lengths and slopes ("rakes") of the stem and stern posts, as well as the positions for the frames (the ship's ribs), which were called "stations." And it showed the heights and spacings of the gun ports, and positions of masts, railings, channels, and wales (the thickest planking on the ship's side).

Directly below the sheer plan appeared the half-breadth plan, which was an overhead view of one-half of the ship's hull lengthwise. Here, the frame stations were repeated, and flowing curves marked positions of equal height above the keel, so that one could see the changing shape of the hull from keel to deck line.

Finally, off to one side, was the body plan. This was a split view, the left side showing the ship from astern and the right from ahead. This plan showed the shapes of the frames progressing from either end of the ship toward the main frame, the broadest frame in the ship.

Creation of the scale draft began with the keel length decided , the beam (width), and the location of the main frame on the keel. Having established these, the naval architect proceeded to develop his three plans simultaneously, drawing in an item on one, then transferring it to each of the others to ensure harmony and unity before going on with another. You might think of it as building a house of bricks, where, after laying each brick, you inspected it from the side, the top, and both ends to be sure it was harmonious in all planes and would fulfill its purpose in that position in the total structure. The test for one of these drafts was that, except for the keel, every line in it should appear straight in two views and smoothly curved in the third.

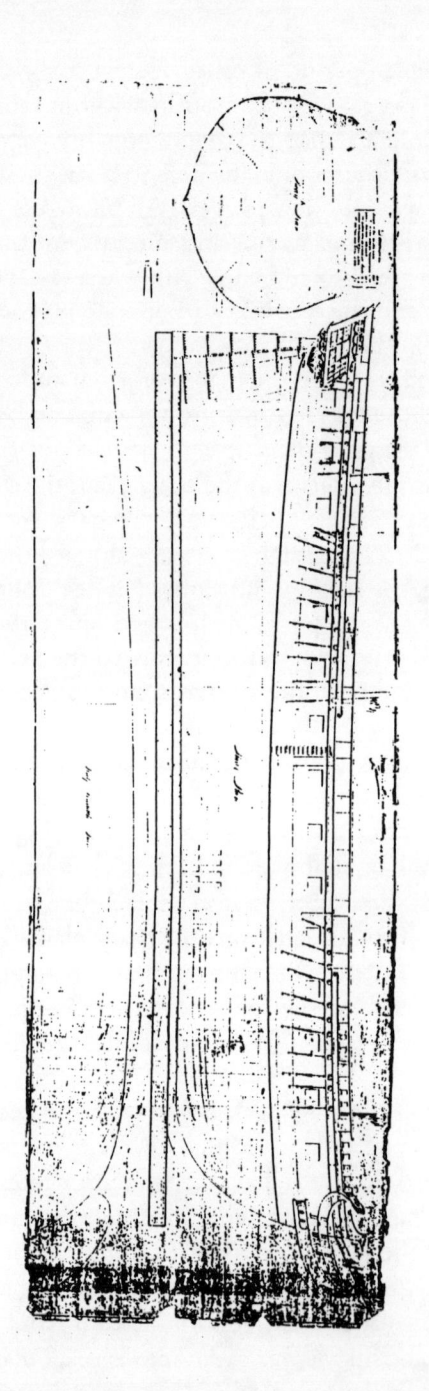

Original builder's draught for frigate CONSTITUTION.

Accompanying the draft, was a "table of dimensions," sometimes called the "table of offsets." Here were listed all the ship's major dimensions, together with an item-by-item description of the hundreds of shaped pieces of wood that would go into building the ship, and with some specific directions as to how they ought to be fitted and/or finished. Humphreys also provided an estimate of the quantities of timber necessary, from 50,000 locust treenails in 18-, 24-, and 30-inch lengths, to 18,000 feet of four inch plank for bottom and ceiling planking, to one live oak stern post thirty feet long and twenty-two inches square.

From this single sheet of drawings and the list of materials, shipwrights in six ports would build the first frigates for our Navy. Because of their individual interpretations of the plans, *Constitution* and her "sisters" were similar in appearance, but not identical.

The most innovative elements of Humphreys' design, however, were not to be seen in his half model or in his draft, but were to be found in different places in his materials requirements list and evident only when the ship's structure took shape.

A sailing frigate required 1500 or more trees in its construction, trees shaped into an even greater number of parts that were joined into what was hoped would be a strong, unified structure. But when that structure was over two hundred feet long, was expected to carry large weights even near its extremes, and would exist in the highly dynamic environment of the sea, these various conditions tended to combine to cause the ship — at the very least — to distort into some shape other than that in which it was built. In such warships, the major result was a condition called "hogging," where the ends of the ship bow downward leaving the midpoint of the keel higher than either extreme. This condition is detrimental to the ship's speed and maneuverability, not to mention its longevity.

In the late 18th Century, many of the world's navies commonly used short, heavy pieces of wood attached diagonally over sections of the inner hull to help stiffen it and counteract hogging. Joshua Humphreys, with warship design experience dating back to the Revolution, was aware of this, of course, but he took the idea to an extent never before seen in his new design for a 44-gun frigate.

The "backbone" of the ship is its keel, a single member composed of several interlocked pieces that is nearly as long as the ship finally will be. Across this backbone at intervals are attached the frames, the ship's "ribs," curved like our own ribs to give the final product its shape. In Humphreys' design, these frames fitted over and around the keel, and were clamped to it by the keelson, a near-twin to

Orlop

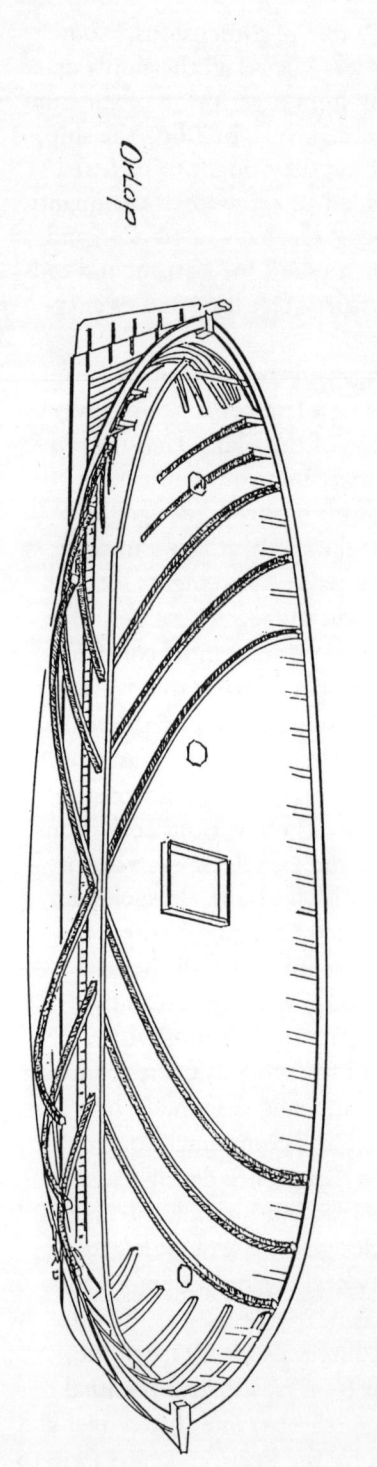

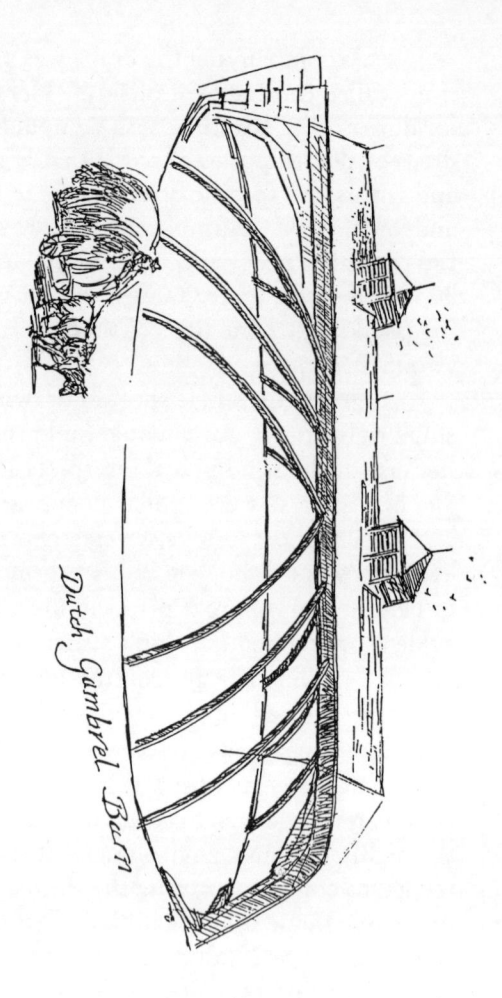

Dutch Gambrel Barn

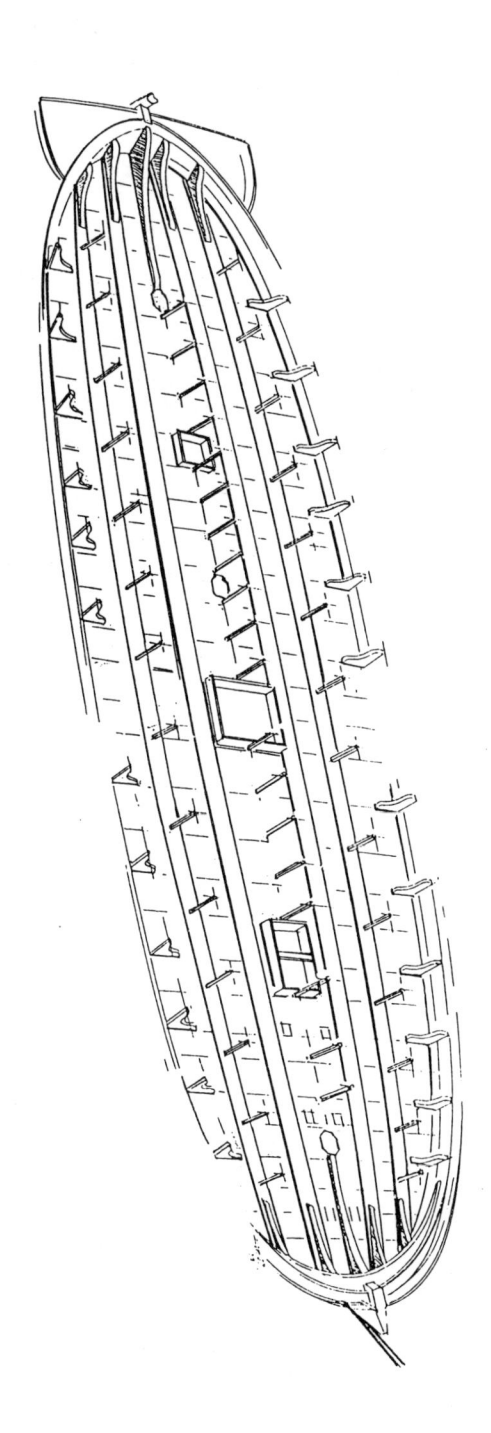

Birth Deck

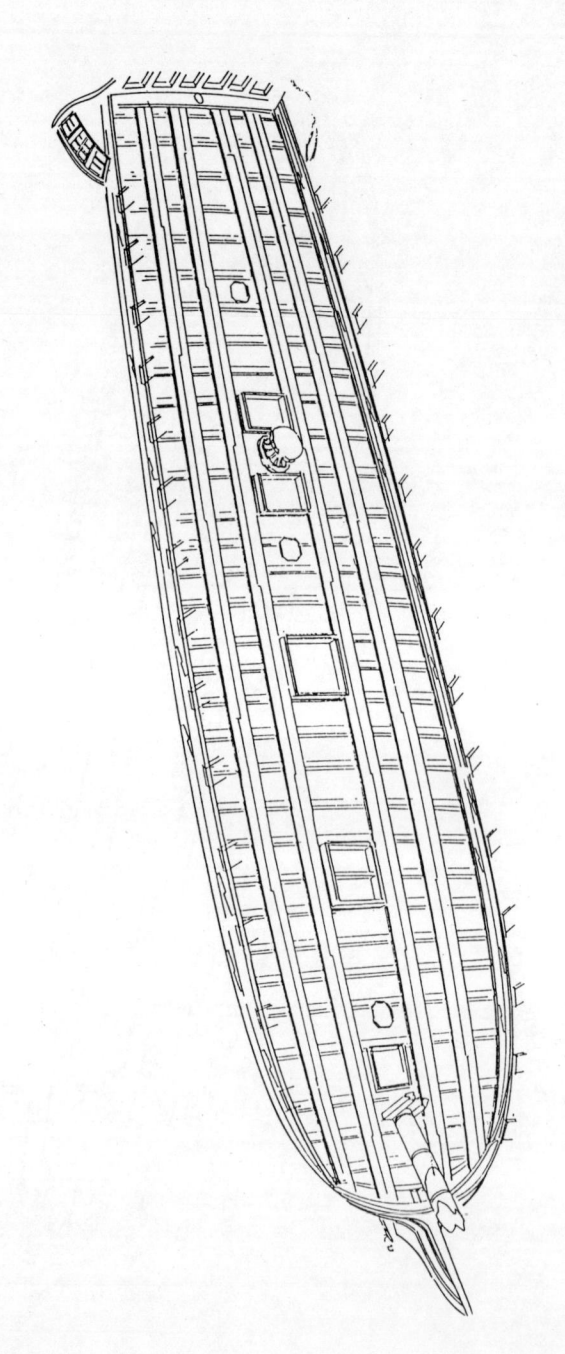

Gun Deck

Upper Deck

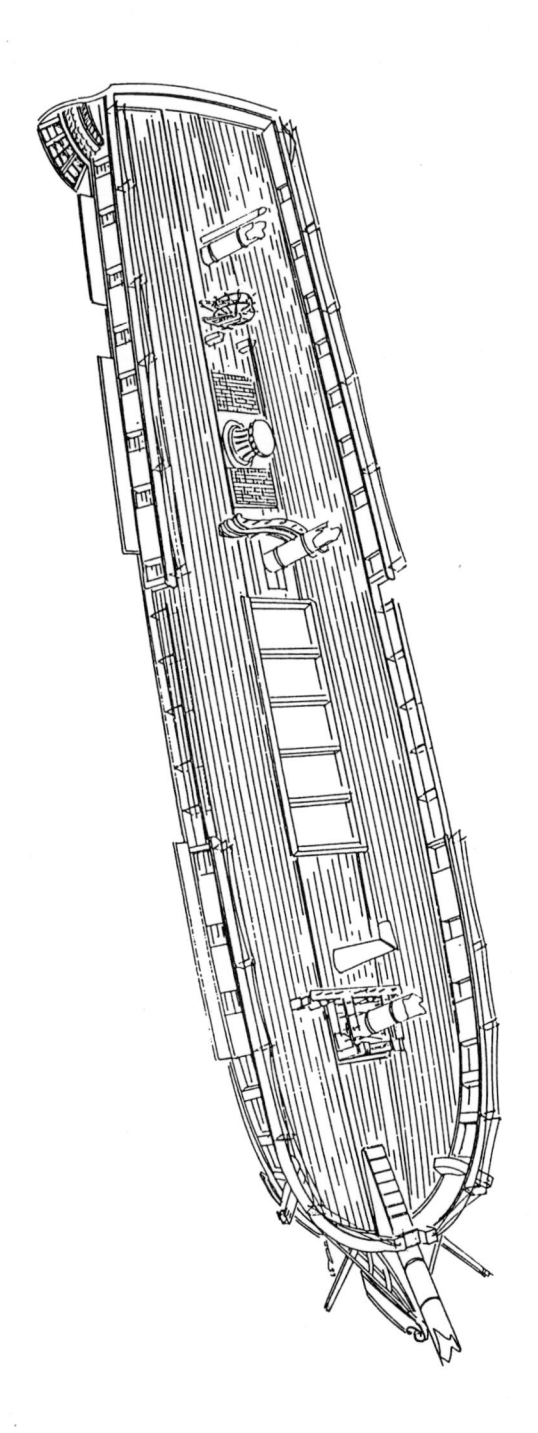

the keel fastened over it throughout their length by stout copper pins more than inch thick and peened over at both ends to hold them securely. The frames themselves consisted of several pieces ("futtocks") laid parallel to one another and pinned together with locust treenails in such a way that no point where the ends of two consecutive futtocks butted together was directly opposite a similar point in the parallel futtocks. In effect, the frames were "sistered" so that each pair presented a unit two feet wide and nearly a foot thick. Humphreys' design allowed just two inches of space between each pair of sistered frames.

On the outside of the vertically rising frames were attached the horizontal wales and planking of the ship's external "skin," with the thickest timbers occurring above the waterline and just below the gun ports. All of these timbers were joined end-to-end. On the inside of the frames, similar horizontal "ceiling" planking was laid. All three layers were united by metal pins driven through them and clinched at both ends for security.

Once the shell of the ship was erected, its volume could be filled in with the necessary decks, etc. At the levels where deck beams would span the interval from side to side, two heavier, thicker strakes of timbers than the ceiling planking, together called a clamp, were installed to support them. Having very quickly erected the lower shell of the frigate, we now come to Joshua Humphreys' innovation.

Returning to the bilges of the ship, we find that the designer called for long, curving pieces of wood called "diagonal riders" to be installed between the keel and the berth deck beams. Three pairs of diagonals in the forward part of the ship and a similar number aft. The rearmost of the forward set of diagonals butted to the keel/keelson and the forwardmost of the after set of diagonals at the ship's midpoint and ran outward, forward and upward to attach to either end of the eighth berth deck beam from the bow. The diagonal next forward began two frames distance forward of the first and ran up to the ends of the sixth deck beam from the bow. The forwardmost pair began yet another two frames distance forward and connected to the fourth deck beam from the bow. The three pairs of after diagonals were mirror images of those just described. Their upper ends connected to the eighth, sixth, and fourth deck beams counted from the stern. The diagonals were through-bolted to the hull at two foot intervals. Other than the midship riders, which butted against each other, all of the others were tenoned into the keelson.

Humphreys also called for the installation of two "transom riders" under the berth deck aft of the diagonal riders, specifying only that they be eighteen feet long and a foot square. They likely were placed parallel to the diagonal riders and perhaps with half the spacing, but precisely where their respective end points were is not known. They were bolted to "every other timber." At the forward extremity of the ship, Humphreys provided five massive breasthooks straddling the stem and keelson from just below the berth deck to immediately aft of the foremast.

Through this system of diagonals, Humphreys was causing the downward thrust of weights at the ends of his frigate in press against one another near the ship's center of bending at the keel, and largely counteracting the detrimental effects. Rough modern model tests found that a load of about 800 pounds would deflect the model's keel almost three-quarters of an inch when Humphreys' diagonals were absent. With them installed, a load of about 2250 pounds similarly applied caused a deflection of less than half an inch. Subsequent computer modelling by the David W. Taylor Ship Research and Development Center at Carderock, Maryland, confirmed the importance of the diagonals in offsetting hogging.

At the berth deck level, Humphreys provided for four pairs of white oak "thick planks" to be installed running the length of the ship. One pair was located on each side of the hatches piercing this deck; the others, farther outboard, midway between the hatches and the ship's hull. Each was five-and-a-half inches thick and at least ten inches wide, the sections lock scarfed together. All were worked to fit over and into the beams and ledges they crossed, and all were firmly attached to the ends of the ship with stout knees[1] of white oak. These, in effect, became an "upper keel," a series of unified members running the ship's entire length at that level.

Also at the berth deck level, Humphreys called for the pieces of the two strakes of "spirketting," the thick pieces occupying the space above the waterways filling the line of jointure of deck beams with the ship's frames, to be "hooked and joggled" into each other. This made them fit like pieces in a jigsaw puzzle, and meant that the spirketting running all around the perimeter of the berth deck became a "fence," tying thick planks, deck beams, and frames into a single large framework. Structurally, all was tied, in turn, to the keel/keelson through the diagonals.

Humphreys further reinforced the berth deck against the strains imposed on it by the presence of the diagonal riders thrusting up under six of its beams by providing a series of standard knees fastened to the ship's sides and, through the deck plank, to the ends of the deck beams below. A total of twelve was provided for each side, so that not only were the beams abutting diagonals reinforced, so, too, was every other beam in the midships area between the upper ends of the midships diagonals.

As innovative and effective as this system is, Humphreys did not stop there. Between the berth deck beams and those of the gun deck above it, he provided for three rows of stanchions, one along the centerline of the ship, and another parallel to it on either side. Each of the outer lines probably was set on the outer row of "thick planks" and under gun deck beams located immediately inboard of gun ports. In other words, a stanchion approximately under each 24-pounder long gun. These stanchions helped to distribute the great weight of these guns (about three-and-a-quarter tons each) throughout the ship's fabric.

Finally, six inch thick "thick planks" were installed in the gun deck in the same pattern followed one deck below, and again attached to the ends of the ship with knees. The spirketting here, too, was hooked and joggled to form a solid perimeter about the deck. The effect of the thick strakes and locked spirketting on this deck and the berth deck was to limit the spreading possible at butt joints. This, in turn, reduced the structure's ability to "droop" at its extremities. A centerline row of movable stanchions helped support the spar deck.

To sum up, Joshua Humphreys' system resulted in a unified gun deck distributing its enormous weight through stanchions to a unified berth deck which, in turn, formed one "side" of a longitudinal girder, triangular in cross-section, further comprised of two sides made of diagonals at whose apex was the ship's eel. This system resulted in the ship having enough flexibility to work easily in a seaway while having the inherent dynamic energy to counteract the natural tendency of a long wooden warship to hog.

Humphreys left no clue as to how he happened upon this innovation. Perhaps a source of inspiration may have been the Dutch-originated "bow roof" incorporating curved beams found in both barns and houses in Pennsylvania. Another may have been the spate of bridge construction occurring in America in the 1790s. Architects of that era had rediscovered the truss systems employed in Europe two centuries and more earlier and were incorporating them into their bridge designs. Diagonals such as Humphreys used were features of both the "queen truss" and "Warren truss" designs of bridges. The normal shape of a ship's hull allowed Humphreys to strengthen the system further by employing pre-stressed timbers for the diagonals. These great baulks of wood, softened in long troughs of boiling salt water and then bent to shape, took on all the characteristics of an

Locking Scarph

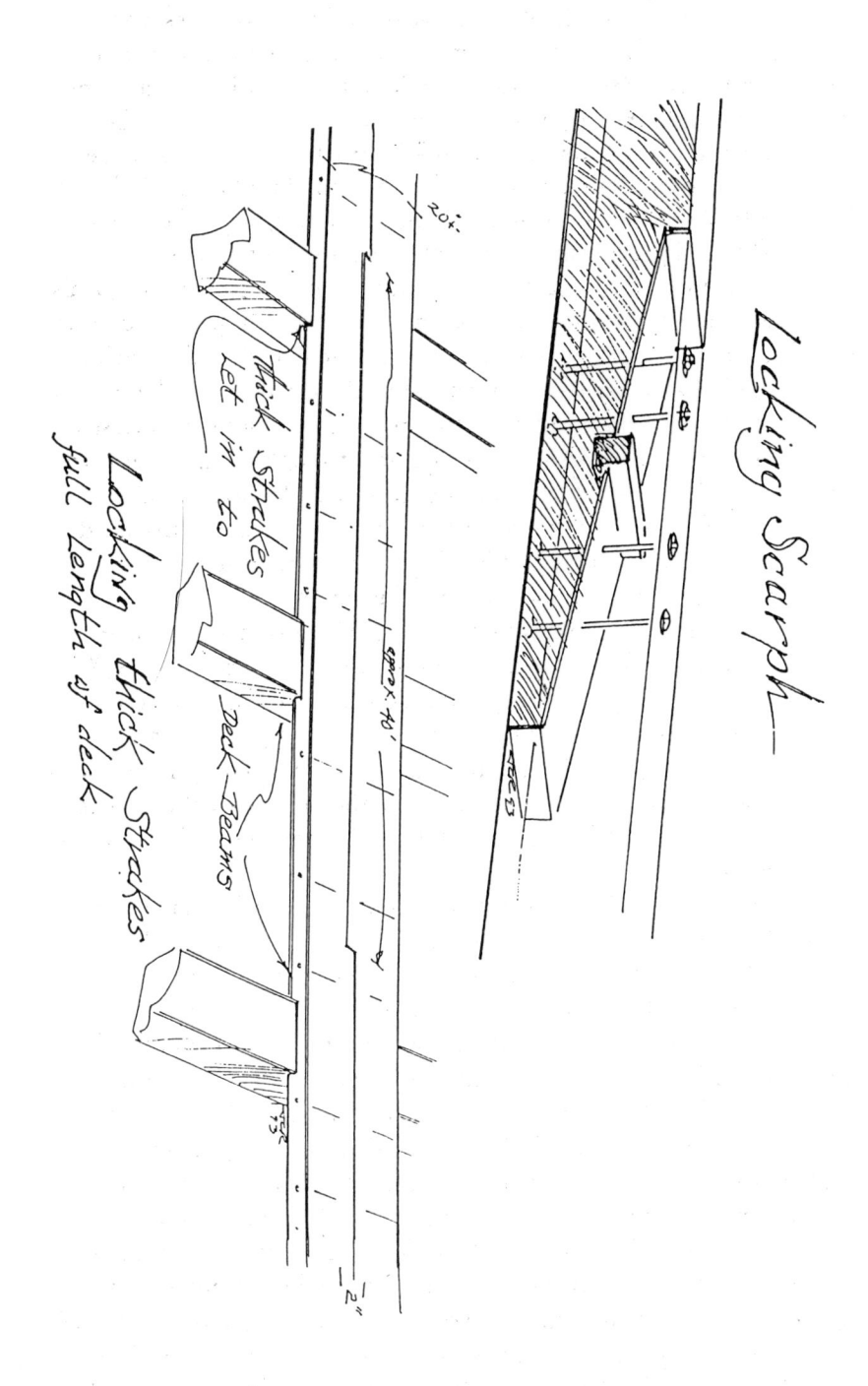

Thick Strakes Let in to Deck Beams

Locking thick strakes full length of deck

archer's bow, resistant to any forces seeking to alter their shapes — particularly on the outside of the curve — and naturally seeking to return to its manufactured shape when any displacement occurred. This desirable trait Humphreys transmitted to his entire structure by through-fastening the diagonals through the total thickness of the ship's fabric at every frame they crossed. Furthermore, his arrangement of diagonals resulted in more than half the hull being reinforced by at least two diagonals. It was a stroke of genius, a novel concept not to be found previously among any nation's shipbuilders.[2]

This integrated structural system with its six pairs of diagonals spanning much of the lower hull, then, is Joshua Humphreys' unique contribution to the art of warship design. The British and French, at least, already had built 44-gun frigates, but the Quaker was the first to employ full length (keel to lower deck beams) one-piece pre-stressed diagonals in his frigate design, and to unify strength members at lower and main deck levels. He not only successfully blended French proportions for speed with British practices for sturdiness, he added a feature which greatly increased his ships' strength, ensuring that their size and power and endurance was no illusion.[3]

As Joshua Humphreys set about getting his ideas on paper, two additional burdens were placed upon him. The Secretary of War directed him, on 21 June, to negotiate a contract for the construction of a building in which the full-size patterns for the principal pieces of the ship, called "moulds," could be laid out and created (These would be first used by the woodcutters to ensure they cut trees of adequate and proper shape, and later by the shipwrights for the final shaping of the actual pieces.)

A short time later, in July, an itinerant English Quaker shipwright by the name of Josiah Fox was hired as a clerk in the War Department and given duties assisting the designer in the preparation of the building plan for the 44s. Fox, ten years younger than Humphreys, had apprenticed as a shipwright in England and, having an independent income, had spent seven years studying at European yards. He had been in America since late October 1793, and may have secured the position through the influence of his cousin, Andrew Endicott, then Surveyor General of the United States.[4] From the outset, Fox sought to make alterations to the design contrary to Humphreys' directions, leading the latter, under pressure from the Secretary of War to "expedite this work," to make the initial drawing himself. He gave it the name "Terrible," meaning "awesome." It was completed by September. Copies for the building yards, as well as moulds, were finally drawn from Humphreys' original by Fox and

William Doughty, clerk at Humphreys' yard, and most were distributed by the end of November.[5]

NOTES:

1. A naturally angled piece of wood, such as might be cut from the area of a tree including a portion of the trunk and the near portion of a large limb. Those involved here were approximately right angles, roughly "L" shaped, the longer "arm" extending horizontally on deck and the shorter one rising against the hull.

2. Humphreys' innovation not only speaks to his genius, it is a testimonial to the American shipwrights' skills in those days. To work, all of the interlocking pieces of this huge "Chinese Puzzle" had to fit together with precision. That the constructors were able to accomplish it is clear evidence of their high technical abilities.

3. Frederick H. af Chapman, the noted Swedish naval architect of the late 18th Century, designed a "privateer frigate" which included a ship-long system of stanchions and diagonals limited to the vertical plane between the keelson and the gun deck. The first British use of diagonals, closer to Humphreys' concept but in a ship of the line, was introduced by Sir Robert Seppings in *Tremendous* (1811). After becoming Surveyor of the Royal Navy in 1813, he altered the diagonals idea into almost a "basket weave" structure, termed a "trussed frame," employing shorter timbers in a crisscross network of reinforcement from keel to berth deck beams against the inner sides of the ship. This probably was forced upon him by the lack of sufficient timbers of adequate size in England, a factor Joshua Humphreys not to consider.

4. Endicott and his brother, Benjamin, later prepared the layout, based upon the proposal of Pierre L'Enfant, used in the construction of Washington, D. C.

5. William P. Bass has done an exhaustive comparison of the *Terrible* drawing and dated, signed drawings by both Fox and Doughty which clearly shows that Humphreys' original hull form was used without variance by his copyists. This, in the present writer's opinion, eliminates Fox from any credit for the design of the 44s. Fox subsequently designed frigates *Crescent* (for Algiers), *Philadelphia*, and *John Adams*, as well as brigs *Wasp* and *Hornet*, and two gunboats. He served as an appointed Naval Constructor from 1804 until 1809, when he was summarily discharged, apparently for political reasons. The success and fame of the 44s only increased the acrimonious relationship between Fox and Humphreys, and it was continued by succeeding generations on both sides. The course of events detailed here is based on contemporary correspondence and records, and ignores later allegations. William Doughty, appointed Naval Constructor in 1813, later designed the liners *Columbus* and those of the *North Carolina* class, together with *Alligator* class sloops, *Argus* and *Wasp* class sloops of war, and gunboats and row galleys. He served until 1837, when he resigned his commission to go into business with his son as a supplier of naval stores. As for Joshua Humphreys himself, his employment as Naval Constructor was terminated on 1 November 1801, when a change of administrations resulted in the cancellation of his 74-gunners and a redirection toward a gunboat navy.

Part III
The Building Team & Contracts

Even as Joshua Humphreys was beginning to shape his model, the President and Secretary Knox were occupied with organizing the construction program. Although it was recognized that economies might be effected by limiting the building sites to one or two, the decision was made to have each of the six vessels built at different locations, in hopes of broadening the nation's shipbuilding experience in the process and, perhaps, in hopes of having all the units available sooner. Recommendations were sought from regional politicians and businessmen, and also considered were the yards' ship building activities during the Revolution.

Within three weeks of signing the bill, President Washington assigned construction of the six frigates to Portsmouth (New Hampshire), Boston, New York, Philadelphia, Baltimore, and Gosport (Portsmouth), Virginia. Contracts were generally let with existing yards at these several places. In Boston, the yard belonging to Edmund Hartt, which was located near where Coast Guard Base Boston stands today, north of Copp's Hill, was selected to build Frigate "B."

Secretary Knox next appointed four-man teams to oversee the building activity at each location on an exclusive, full-time basis. Having little knowledge of other persons who might have the proper credentials for managing the project and safeguarding the Government's interest, he made his selections largely from among those who had been commissioned officers in the Revolution, as he, himself, had been.

The senior man was styled the "Navy Agent." He was responsible for monitoring contract compliance by the shipbuilder, for letting and overseeing local contracts, approving expenditures and making disbursements, supervising the Clerk of the Yard, and for keeping the Secretary apprised of progress and problems. In Boston, the man selected by Knox was 47-year-old Henry Jackson, a major general in the Massachusetts militia. Jackson had been commissioned a colonel in the Continental Army and had commanded three different regiments, seeing combat in Rhode Island and New Jersey. For his efforts as Navy Agent, he would receive a two-and-a-half percent commission on the sums expended.

(In 1797, Jackson would be succeeded as Navy Agent by the wealthy merchant Stephen Higginson. The latter had been a successful privateer in the Revolution and later the second in command of a militia regiment sent to put down Shay's Rebellion. His fortune may have been in excess of half a million dollars at the time of his appointment.)

Second senior on the team was Captain Samuel Nicholson, Sr., 51, whose commission in the U. S. Navy dated from 4 June 1794 — also the second senior officer in the service. He had been a captain in the Continental Navy, and had commanded the sloop *Dolphin* and later frigate *Deane*. His successes in the Revolution included the taking of three British sloops of war. At this later period, he was to provide the operational expertise to ensure that the new ship would fulfill her mission — even to directing minor modifications to Humphreys design where he thought necessary. His annual salary was $900 plus the cash equivalent of the cost of six rations a day: about $75.

The "Naval Constructor" was George Claghorn, 46, another militia officer who had fought at Bunker Hill and been wounded. He had been a colonel at war's end, and continued to use the title. Subsequent to independence, he had been a shipbuilder at New Bedford, Massachusetts, and in 1785 had launched the *Rebecca* of 175 tons, said to have been the first American whaler to double Cape Horn for a cargo of oil. It was to be his job to oversee the actual construction of the ship, establishing priorities, deciding hirings and firings, and ensuring the quality of workmanship and correctness of procedures. His pay would be $2000 a year.

Working directly for the Navy Agent was the "Clerk of the Yard" (also referred to as "Store Keeper"). Caleb Gibbs, 39, who had held the rank of Continental Army major, commanded George Washington's Guard in the Revolution, and had since been a merchant, was the man chosen. For $750 a year, he would receive and maintain inventories of the supplies and equipment acquired by both Federal and local contracts, make issues to the builders or, later, the ship, with the Navy Agent's approval, and keep the account ledgers, making periodic reports to Secretary Knox and the Treasury. (Of all the initial appointees, Gibbs was the longest in his position, retaining it until his death in November 1818.)

At the time the "Act to provide a naval armament" was signed by President Washington, no funds were appropriated to pay for the construction of the six ships authorized. Indeed, nothing existed that could be immediately used in their creation. As Secretary of War Knox was to write later:

> "...few or no materials of any sort, either for construction or equipment, existed in their proper shape... Everything, if not to be created, was to be modified... The wood of which the frames were to be made was standing in the forests; the iron for the cannon lying in its natural bed; and the flax and hemp, perhaps in their seed..."

Recognizing that funding would be forthcoming, Knox and Secretary of the Treasury Alexander Hamilton, who had responsibility for letting contracts, took preliminary steps to be ready to act when monies were available. Joshua Humphreys provided the materials specifications:

> "...it was agreed that the frames should be of live oak and red cedar; that is, the stern post, and all the stern frames, the upper piece of the stem, and all the frames, (except the lower piece) the first, second, and third futtocks, three-fourths of the top-timber, stanchions, counter-timbers, bow-timbers, howse-pieces, night-heads, breast-hooks, partners for masts and knees, all of live oak; and one-fourth of the top timbers, the half top timbers, and half counter-timbers, of red cedar... Floor timbers...of live oak... The keel, keelson, beams, ledges, plank for the sides, bottom, ceiling, deck-plank under the guns, deadwoods, lower piece stem, and wales, of the best white oak; decks of the best Carolina pitch pine...
>
> "Copper was considered a very essential component..."

The selection of live oak for key elements of the ship's framework was both wise and fraught with problems. In the century and a half colonials had been building their own ships, the durable properties of the wood had become well known: not only was it most rot-resistant, it also was more resistant to boring pests. Off-setting its benefits were the facts that it only grew in marshy, pestilential areas where transport was nearly impossible, it was difficult to saw and shape, and it was very heavy. The U. S. Navy used a planning figure of 70.5 pounds per cubic foot for live oak as opposed to 54 for white. Cedar and pine, the other two major woods used, ran about half these weights.

Discussion between the War and Treasury Departments began 4 April concerning the procurement of materials. On the 16th, the latter office issued advertisements for live oak and cedar timber, as well as for cannon balls, 24-pounder cannon, and kentledge. Additional advertisements were published for yellow and pitch pine, white oak, and locust treenails on 7 May.

On 9 June 1794, $688,888.32 were appropriated for initial construction costs. That same day, a contract was let with John T. Morgan, a master shipwright of Boston, for him to proceed to Charleston and Savannah to procure the necessary live oak, red cedar, and pitch pine materials. He was to search for the timber, superintend its cutting and forming by the moulds, and arrange for its shipment to the six ports where the frigates were to be built. For his services, he was to be paid $2000 annually. (And on an optimistic note, should it be subsequently decided to build a frigate at Charleston, Mr. Morgan would be the builder.) Daniel Stephens and Isaac Holmes of Charleston were appointed agents to assist Morgan in administering contracts in North and South Carolina, while John Habersham and Joseph Clay of Savannah performed that function in Georgia.

A week after this, the Treasury Department directed its Collector of Customs at New London, Connecticut, Jedidiah Huntington, to procure sixty axmen and thirty ship carpenters from Connecticut, Rhode Island, and the "western coast of Massachusetts" to be sent south to cut the trees. Huntington also was required to arrange for the procurement and shipment of supporting supplies and provisions from New London, New York, and Philadelphia, wherever the goods could be had at the most economic price.

The Secretary of the Treasury, on 25 June, received estimates of the composition metal, sheathing copper, bolts, nails, bunting, and iron kitchens ("cambooses") needed. Many of these were to be ordered in England, through our Minister in London, as such items were not readily available in the new United States. It was considered possible to procure suitable anchors on this side of the Atlantic and, indeed, an advertisement for bids on the whole range of sizes needed was sent to twenty-six addressees on 30 June. Nearly three months later, contracts for anchors ranging in size from 3.5 to 50 hundredweight (the principal anchors for the 44-gun frigates) were awarded to Nathaniel Cushing and Hodijah Dallies of Pembroke and Dighton, Massachusetts, respectively, and an Elijah Phelps. On the following Christmas Eve, further contracts, each for 50 and 44 hundredweight anchors, were issued to Cushing and Solomon Townsend of New York. In Cushing's case, they were to be delivered to Boston, and one of 6,116 pounds cast by him in January 1798 is known to have been delivered to the ship.

The first cannon contract was let on 28 June. The Cecil Iron Works of Maryland was to provide ninety of the 24-pounders required for the frigates, together with additional 32- and 24-pounders for Army forts, at $121.66 per ton. All were to be delivered by 1 January 1795.

In the interests of economy, it was decided that the Navy Agents previously appointed by Secretary Knox also would attend to local Treasury interests concerning contracts. Accordingly, on 5 and 7 July instructions were sent to them by that Department to procure all white oak, yellow pine, and treenails meeting specifications in their immediate areas. It was expected that a surer, and cheaper, supply thereby could be gained. On 15 July, they received further instructions to procure masts, blocks, ironwork, cooperage, cordage, and sailcloth from local sources.

Levi Hollingsworth, Son, and Company, of New Jersey and Pennsylvania, were awarded a contract for cannon balls and kentledge on 9 July. To be provided were ninety-two tons of balls at $37.33 per ton and 198 tons of the iron ballast, to have a hole in either end "for hooking," at $28.66 per ton. (This contract was increased to 340 tons of ballast later in the year.) A second contract for cannon balls and kentledge went to J. J. Faesch and Company, of New Jersey, on 28 July, calling for ninety-eight tons of the former and 256 tons of the latter at the same prices. Henry Jackson was authorized to purchase for his frigate, at the reduced price of $25 per ton, some 150 tons of foreign kentledge in the possession of an unnamed Boston citizen.

On 23 July, a contract was let with Paul Revere for the casting of ten 8-inch brass howitzers. James Byers in Springfield, Massachusetts, received a like order. Using government-supplied tin and copper, they were to cast the weapons for seventeen cents a pound, finished weight (around 1700 pounds each). Revere was to deliver his first pair to a wharf in Boston six weeks after the delivery of the metals, and at least one pair per month thereafter. Each piece was to bear the raised "Arms of the United States" and "Dolphins." All twenty were delivered by the end of 1795.

The second contract for sixty 24-pounder naval cannon and additional numbers of fortress guns was signed on 8 August with Furnace Hope in Providence, Rhode Island. Delivery was to be completed by 1 May 1795 at a price of $106.66 per ton. (The order for the remaining thirty naval guns was withheld from both Cecil Iron Works and Furnace Hope in the expectation that one of the thirteen other foundries receiving advertisements would qualify for it. This, however, did not come about, and Cecil eventually got the order.)

Within a few months it became apparent that both the Government and the contractors had been overly optimistic concerning the industrial capability to produce acceptable large caliber weapons on the agreed schedule. While Furnace Hope was meeting it with some success, the Cecil Iron Works was stumbling badly. When Secretary Knox's successor, Timothy Pickering, reported on the matter to Congress nearly eighteen months later, he wrote:

> "The casting of cannon has not been attended, hitherto, with the expected success. The foundries which formerly succeeded very well in the casting of small guns, were not at all well adapted to the casting of 24...pounders. A French gentleman, of some knowledge and experience in cannon foundries, has lately been employed to amend the process of casting, and to improve the machinery of boring; and there is room to hope that his projected improvements will be realized.[1] Nevertheless, in an undertaking so important, and, at the same time, so expensive, it was desirable to obtain, if possible, a complete cannon founder; and, from the information received, it seemed probable that one might be procured from one of the best founders in Europe. Measures, for that purpose, have accordingly been taken."[2]

No further cannon contracts were let until October 1796, when it became necessary to order the batteries for a tribute frigate then being built for the Algerines. Given that impetus, on the 25th of that month, a contract was awarded to the Cecil Iron Works for 9- and 6-pounders needed for the corsair *Crescent*, together with the remaining 24-pounders and the 12-pounders planned for the American units. The price had risen to $133.25 per ton. These delays in contracting and delivery later would cause Captain Nicholson, for one, to take unusual measures in arming his frigate.

Gardner and Olden of Philadelphia received the final ballast contracts on 20 August 1794 and 3 February 1795: one hundred tons of kentledge in each order.

While all contracting activity was transpiring in Philadelphia and northward, Habersham and Clay were busy in Georgia. At Savannah, on 2 September, an agreement was made for live oak (quercus virginiana) at the rate of six cents (Georgia money) per foot. The wood was to be cut by the United States, but hauled to water for shipment by the contractors. (The contractors later proved to be unable to provide the transport, and the Treasury Department made arrangements for oxen, forage, and timber wheels to be sent South after enough live oak for one frigate had been accumulated.)

During September, too, the Boston Manufacturing Company received a contract to manufacture "one entire suit of sails" for each frigate, contrary to earlier directives to the Naval Agents. The price agreed upon reportedly was between $13 and $15 per 39-yard bolt. Production was completed before the year ended.[3]

The axmen and carpenters hired in New England had yet to arrive on the scene. Because the appropriations bill had not cleared until June, which was the onset of the sickeningly hot climate on the malarial sea islands of Georgia, home to the live oak, it had been decided that they should await the coming of cooler weather. Finally, on 23 September, the group headed South.

Captain John Barry of Revolutionary War fame, and captain-designate of the frigate building in Philadelphia, was sent to Georgia on 5 October in the brig *Schuylkill*, to learn first-hand the situation and to get things begun expeditiously. On the 14th, he arrived at Gascoigne's Bluff on the northwest coast of St. Simon's Island, where he soon located John Morgan and learned that work had not yet begun. The next day a shipment of tools, some of the provisions, and some of the moulds arrived. By the 20th, sixteen Black hands had been secured from Messrs. Spaulding and Cooper, local landowners. With them, Morgan began preparatory clearing operations on the lands of Richard Leake about the Bluff. Eighty Yankee woodcutters finally arrived on the 22nd and spent that day building rude shelters for themselves. On 23 October 1794, the cutting of live oak for the frigates was begun. By the 28th, Morgan reported to Barry that he thought the first shipload of timbers, consigned to the Philadelphia frigate, would be ready to be put aboard ship about 4 November; others would be ready as the ships could be hired and brought to the island for loading.

(A tradition has it that the first tree felled for *Constitution* was an immense live oak to be used for her stern post. It was reported to have come from Cannon's Point, at the north end of St. Simon's. The stump of this tree was said to have been banded in iron bearing the inscription "U. S. Frigate *Constitution*, 1794," and allegedly was on display at the International Cotton Exhibition in Atlanta, Georgia, in 1895, but this cannot be substantiated.)

Captain Barry, satisfied with the beginning made, was back in Philadelphia by 10 November, and in an 18 December letter to the Secretary of War, he was reporting that one shipload already had been delivered to that city, and that others were soon to follow, bound for there and the other building sites.

On 22 December, the Commissioner of the Revenue, Tench Coxe, reported to Alexander Hamilton that a second group of axmen, twenty in number from Delaware, was about to sail for Georgia. Thus, at the close of 1794, nine months after the frigates had been authorized, plans and moulds had been completed and distributed, the materials for their construction and outfitting had been ordered, and some were beginning to arrive at the shipyards.

NOTES:

1. The "French gentleman" appears to have been one Monsieur DeRancy, who was directed to go to the Cecil Iron Works in July 1794 to show them how to bore cannon. There was also, however, an F. Da Costa who proceeded from Philadelphia to Boston in late June 1795 with a letter of introduction from Colonel of Artillery Stephen Rochefontaine to Paul Revere requesting his assistance in making a demonstration model cannon with which manufacturers could be trained in a new method of casting. Da Costa and Rochefontaine are known to have represented the War Department at the proofing of at least some of the Furnace Hope 24-pounders in Rhode Island.

2. The later presence and activity of the English iron founder Henry Foxall may have been a direct result of these "measures." Foxall arrived at Philadelphia in 1797 and promptly established the Eagle Iron Works in partnership with Robert Morris, Jr., son of the famous Revolutionary War financier. The Works

are said principally to have been occupied with War and Navy Department contracts, although none have been found by the present writer. This report, and the very speed with which an alien established himself in business with a prominent citizen implies high level interest and influence. Furthermore, when the Federal Government moved to Washington in 1800, Foxall was invited to move with it and establish a cannon foundry, just as Pickering had desired in his 1795 letter. There can be no doubt of government interest in the project when it is known that Foxall received a contract for $20,000 worth of 24-, 18- and 12-pounders four days before he bought the first parcel of land for what would become the Columbia Iron Works in Georgetown, D. C. The Works continued to be a prime supplier of guns to the Navy until after the War of 1812, when Foxall sold the business and returned to England.

3. The flaxen canvas necessary to make a suit of sails for each frigate consisted of the following weights and quantities:

#1	100 bolts	#5	82.5 bolts
#2	5 bolts	#6	20 bolts
#3	7.5 bolts	#7	10 bolts
#4	32.5 bolts		

Each bolt was 40 yards long and 20 inches wide, and weighed from 42 pounds (#1) to 23 pounds (#7) per bolt. Cotton canvas was used for studdingsails and all ancillary uses, such as awnings, hammocks cloths, etc. It came in 50 yard bolts of the same width. Canvas for hammocks also came in 50 yard bolts, but was 42 inches wide.

Part IV
Building The Ship

BUILDING THE SHIP

The frigate was built on a slip laid for the purpose in Edmund Hartt's shipyard in the North End of Boston, approximately at the eastern end of the present-day Coast Guard Base. While neither Hartt nor the Constructor, George Claghorn, has left us a description, its features were common to all builders of large vessels. On the sloping shore, as they waited for the first loads of live and white oak to appear, the builders prepared an area of compacted rubble paved with compacted gravel. Set into this "floor" at intervals of five or six feet, parallel to the shore and centered on a line perpendicular to it, were large pieces of timber secured by stakes. These were the foundations for large blocks of oak, more than a foot thick and two or three feet wide, which, in turn, were topped by the "splitting blocks" of clear-grained timber. The "splitting blocks" would bear the weight of the growing ship until shortly before her launch.

The winter of 1794-5 proved to be a bad one. Incessant rain fell in Georgia, inundating the already swampy areas where the live oak grew, and bringing cutting operations to a standstill. Persistent effort resulted in some moulded timbers being shipped out by spring, but the quantities were small and of these, one shipload (bound for New York) was lost in a storm enroute. By June 1795, all but three of the axmen had given up and returned North. These three hardy souls, with a gang of black laborers, strove to keep the supply coming. They reported to Joshua Humphreys that they hoped to complete their operations by May of 1796.

With this dim outlook for supplies, and yet recognizing the need to bring a navy into being, it was decided by the Secretary of War to concentrate the earliest deliveries of live oak, cedar, and yellow pine in the yards at Philadelphia and Baltimore. Slowness of communication partially aborted this plan, in that shipments already had been made by the cutters in Georgia to Boston, Portsmouth, and Gosport. In addition, suppliers in Massachusetts and New Hampshire already had provided the Boston yard with white oak for the frigate's hull planking and tall white pines for her masts.[1] The advent of a new Secretary of War, Timothy Pickering, on 1 January 1795, also contributed to the plan's demise.

Not long after Pickering took office – on 14 March, to be exact – he gave President Washington a list of ten suggested names for the new ships, "such as have occurred in my conversations with gentlemen on the subject." Five of these names, *Constitution* among them, were ultimately selected for hulls already under construction.[2]

Although some of the most important timber — the live oak — was slow in arriving, other kinds of available timber allowed a small number of shipwrights to begin the process of moulding (shaping) raw trees into the forms that would be needed. Carolina pitch pine and white oak deck planking timber was arriving in quantity: enough so that three pairs of sawyers were employed cutting it to size and stacking it in layers to season in open air. Red cedar was being shaped into top timbers, half top timbers, and half counter timbers. Locust was being cut and shaped into the thousands of treenails required to fasten the ship together. Other than the growing assemblage of supplies, little was to be seen in the Hartt yard until the end of May when, at long last, the four stout pieces of white oak which would form the keel arrived from New Jersey. During the summer, these were shaped according to Humphreys' directions and laid atop the splitting blocks on the ways. Held in alignment by treenails driven diagonally into the splitting blocks, each of their locking scarfs were through-bolted with five one-and-one-eighth inch copper bolts from Paul Revere's foundry, and the ends clenched over copper rings. A vee-shaped "rabbet" was cut in either side of the keel's length to take the edge of the garboard strake, the lowest line of hull planking.

As the months passed, more and more live oak arrived and was worked into floor pieces and futtocks. The process of assembling the frames that would give the future legend her shape began. The stern frame was cut and assembled and the pieces that would form the stem shape were also cut.

THE LIMBS OF A TREE

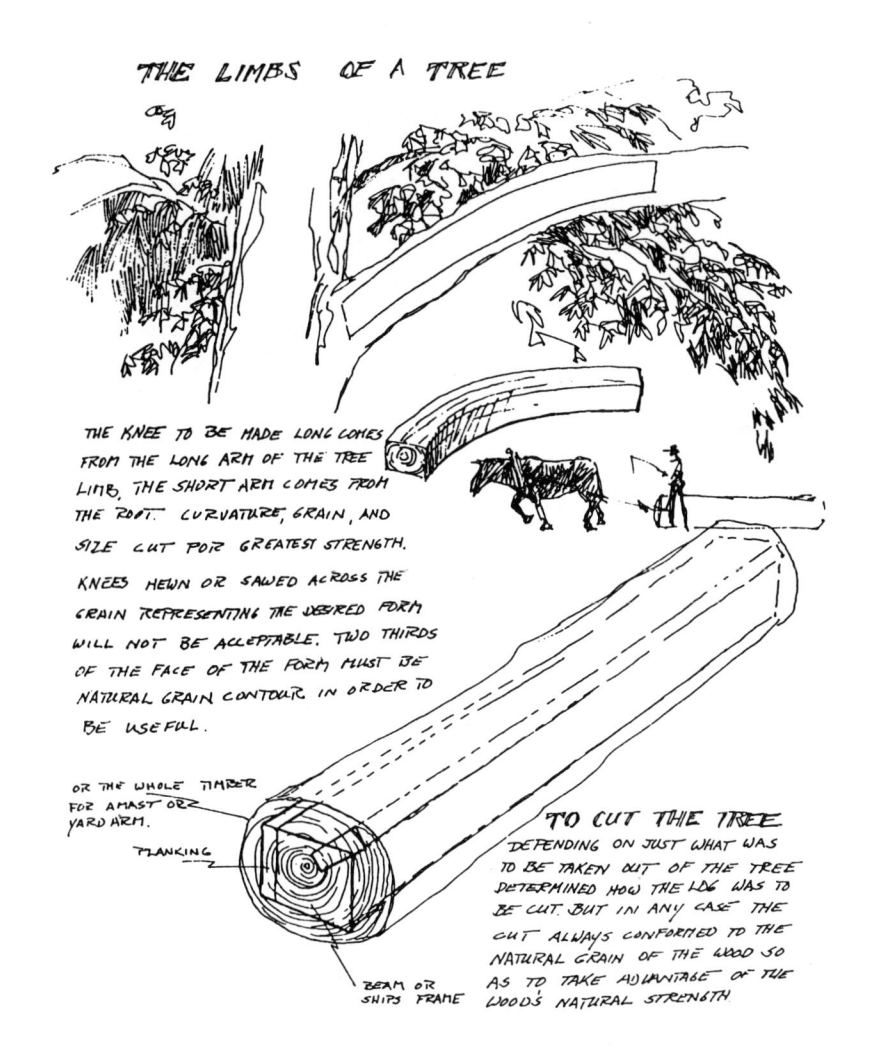

THE KNEE TO BE MADE LONG COMES FROM THE LONG ARM OF THE TREE LIMB. THE SHORT ARM COMES FROM THE ROOT. CURVATURE, GRAIN, AND SIZE CUT FOR GREATEST STRENGTH.

KNEES HEWN OR SAWED ACROSS THE GRAIN REPRESENTING THE DESIRED FORM WILL NOT BE ACCEPTABLE. TWO THIRDS OF THE FACE OF THE FORM MUST BE NATURAL GRAIN CONTOUR IN ORDER TO BE USEFUL.

OR THE WHOLE TIMBER FOR A MAST OR YARD ARM.

PLANKING

BEAM OR SHIPS FRAME

TO CUT THE TREE

DEPENDING ON JUST WHAT WAS TO BE TAKEN OUT OF THE TREE DETERMINED HOW THE LOG WAS TO BE CUT. BUT IN ANY CASE THE CUT ALWAYS CONFORMED TO THE NATURAL GRAIN OF THE WOOD SO AS TO TAKE ADVANTAGE OF THE WOOD'S NATURAL STRENGTH.

THE KNEE

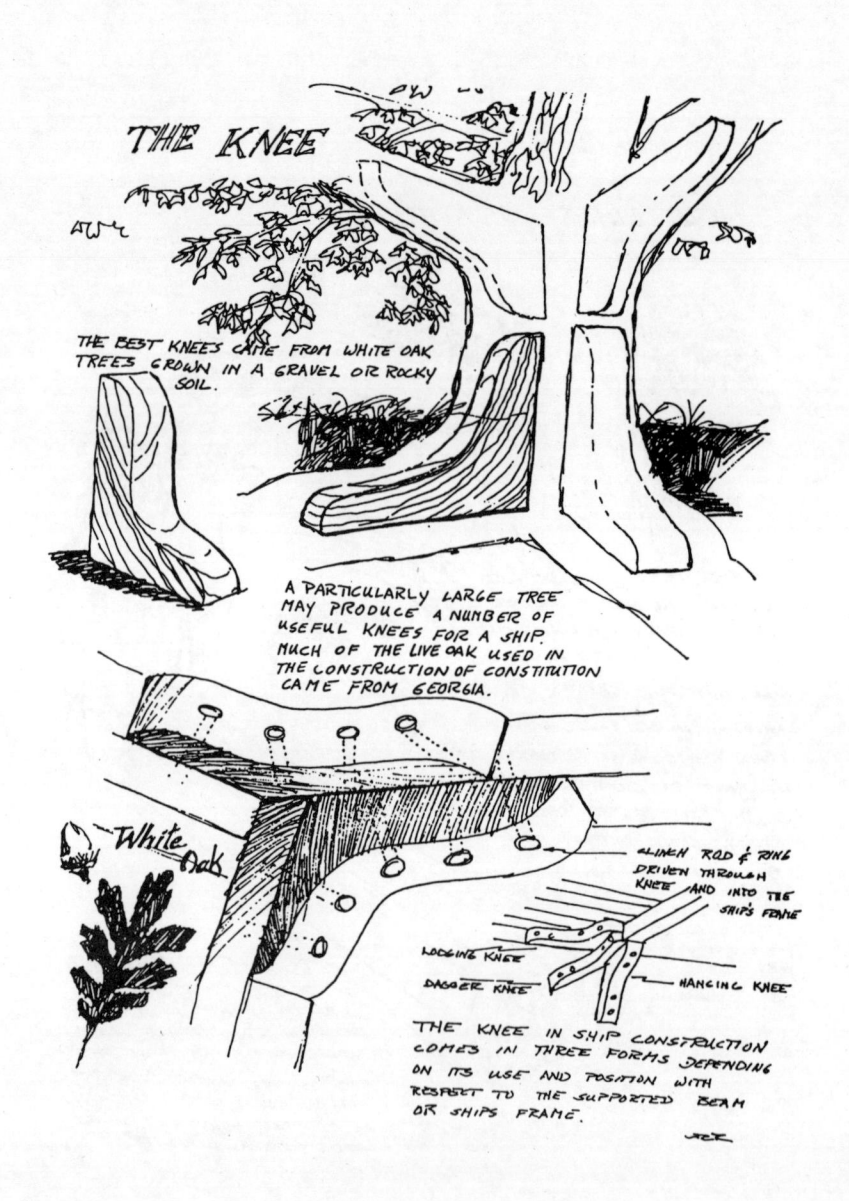

THE BEST KNEES CAME FROM WHITE OAK TREES GROWN IN A GRAVEL OR ROCKY SOIL.

A PARTICULARLY LARGE TREE MAY PRODUCE A NUMBER OF USEFUL KNEES FOR A SHIP. MUCH OF THE LIVE OAK USED IN THE CONSTRUCTION OF CONSTITUTION CAME FROM GEORGIA.

White Oak

CLINCH ROD & RING DRIVEN THROUGH KNEE AND INTO THE SHIP'S FRAME

LODGING KNEE
DAGGER KNEE
HANGING KNEE

THE KNEE IN SHIP CONSTRUCTION COMES IN THREE FORMS DEPENDING ON ITS USE AND POSITION WITH RESPECT TO THE SUPPORTED BEAM OR SHIPS FRAME.

By early December, Humphreys was able to report to Pickering about the frigate which was to be named *Constitution*:

> "The keel is completed and laid on the blocks. The pieces are scarfed and bolted to each other in the best manner. The stern frame is now completing, and will be soon ready to raise. The stem is also putting together, every part being worked to the moulds. About two-thirds of the live oak timbers have been received, and are all worked agreeable to the moulds; great part of those timbers are bolted together in frames, and are ready to put into the ship, but some of the principal pieces for the frames have not yet arrived. All the gun deck and lower deck beams are procured and ready for delivery, and the plank for those decks are received into the yard. The plank for the outside and ceiling are also received and are now seasoning. The copper is all in the public stores. The masts, bowsprit, yards, and other spars, all are ready for working. The bits [sic] for the cables, coamings for the hatchways, partners for the masts, are all ready. The caboose, with a forge, hearth, armorer's tools, spare coppers, boilers, etc., are all complete. Most of the ironwork is in great forwardness. All the necessary contracts are entered into by agent, and the articles contracted for are arriving daily."

Humphreys' terse report did not take note of the suppliers of the many materials being assembled. Aside from the woodcutters in half a dozen states, foundries in Maryland, New Jersey, and Rhode Island were producing cannon and shot. In Boston, Paul Revere had provided the copper bolts and fastenings from his own works; the Skillens brothers, John and Simeon, were carving the Hercules figurehead at their shop on Skillens wharf;[3] Ephraim Thayer was preparing "fire engines" and gun carriages; and the flaxen sails were being cut and sewn at the Old Granary Building, the only loft in the city large enough for the task.

The snail's pace at which construction everywhere was proceeding also caught the attention of the Fourth Congress. A Select Committee, headed by Josiah Parker of Virginia, issued a report shortly before Christmas which recommended the completion only of one 44 guns and one of 36. Surplus perishable goods were to be sold and excess hardware placed in storage. Because of other activities attracting the legislators' attention, nothing ever came of the proposal, although it was pending for months.

Thick strakes

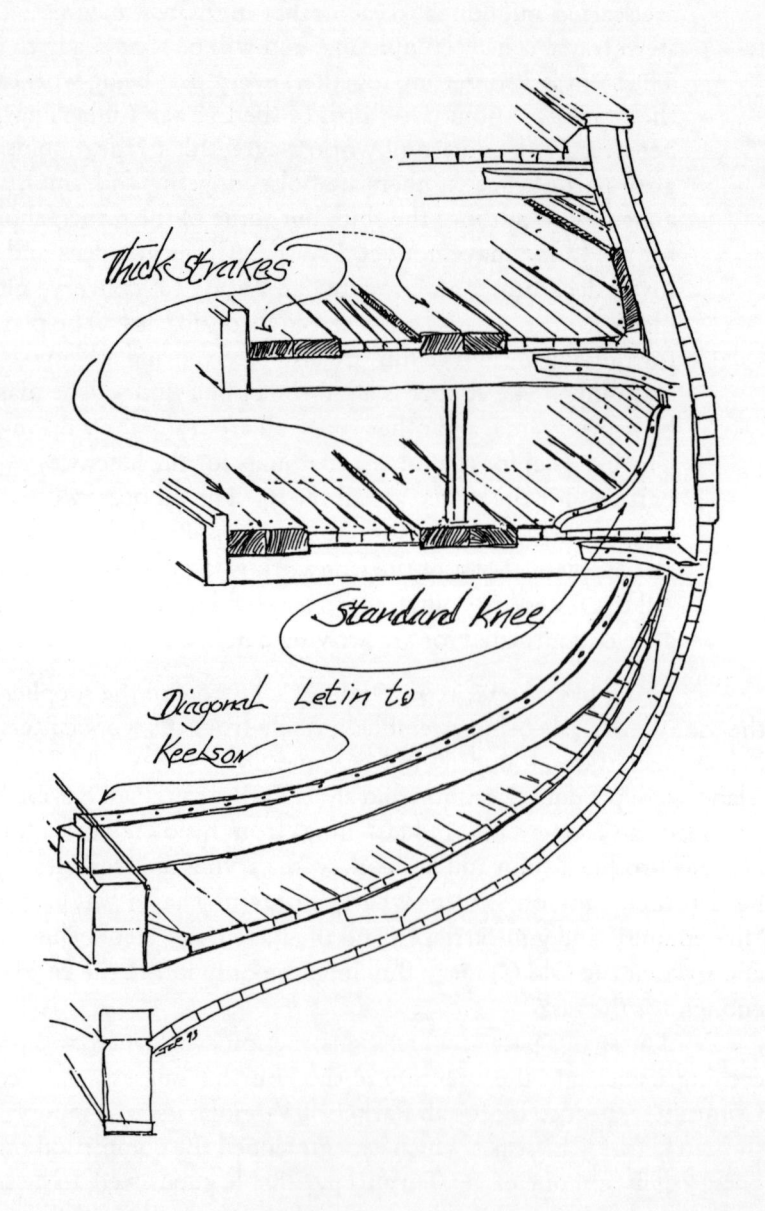

Standard Knee

Diagonal Let in to Keelson

Note that Article Nine of the authorizing Act of 1794 provided for the cessation of all construction should an Algerine peace treaty be secured. Early in March 1796, word was received from the Consul, Joel Barlow, that such a treaty had, indeed, been signed. On 15 March, President Washington communicated to the Congress as follows:

> "The peace...having taken place, it is incumbent upon the Executive to suspend all orders respecting the building of the frigates, procuring materials for them, or preparing materials already obtained, which may be done without intrenching upon contracts or agreements made and entered into before this event.
>
> "But, inasmuch as the loss which the public would incur might be considerable from the dissipation of work men, from certain works or operations being suddenly dropped or left unfinished, and from the derangement in the whole system, consequent upon an immediate suspension of all proceedings under it, I have, therefore, thought it advisable, before taking such a step, to submit the subject to the Senate and House of Representatives, that such measures may be adopted in the premises as may best comport with the public interest."

In the Senate, a committee headed by Federalist William Bingham of Pennsylvania, received the President's letter for consideration and reported only two days later that the President should be authorized "to cause to be completed, with all convenient expedition, two of the said frigates of forty-four, and one of thirty-six guns," using such of the monies as remained from the original appropriation (about $229,000) as well as any available from some $80,000 appropriated for the construction of galleys. The committee also proposed that the President be given discretionary powers to complete the other three frigates "having due regard to the existing price of labor and materials." The Senate passed a bill with all these provisions on 28 March, and it was on the House calendar for debate the next day. That body, after some debate, passed an amended version on 19 April. None of the Bingham committee proposals had been altered. On 20 April 1796, President Washington directed completion of the three frigates "building at Philadelphia, Boston, and Baltimore." Three days later, the order was sent by the War Department to Colonel Claghorn.

As spring became summer, and the politicians warmed to the task of determining a successor to George Washington, construction picked up in Boston. After many months of anticipation, the citizens began to see a ship really taking shape on the apparently long-dormant ways.

The first element to be raised above the keel was the stem, which consisted of two pieces of wood, the lower white oak, joined by a four foot scarf with three copper bolts like those used in the keel. Rabbets were cut in either side of it to take the butt ends of hull planking later on. Next, the apron, which would act as a fillet between the stem and the keel, was fayed (faired or fitted) to the inside of the lower end of the stem. The unit was then transported to the head of the ways, where a pair of sheer legs had been erected, straddling the forward end of the keel.[4] Tackles from the sheer legs to either side of the balance point of the stem assembly were used to lift it off the ground and above the keel end. Another tackle attached high up on the stem was used to haul it into its correct vertical alignment. Once all lined up, all tackles were eased together to lower the assembly and fit it into the scarf at the head of the keel. Shores and treenails held it in position while the through bolts were driven and clenched. "Deadwood" (additional filleting) was then added to strengthen the union of stem/apron to the keel.

While this was going on, another group of shipwrights was creating the stern, consisting of the stern post, wing transom, lower transoms, and fashion pieces. As it ultimately would support the rudder, this vital assembly was hewn from live oak. All of these pieces were transported to the building ways, where a second set of sheer legs was erected over the after end of the keel. Here, they were assembled into a single unit which, once in place, would define the shape of the extreme stern in the vertical plane. The lower end of the sternpost had a tenon cut into it one-third the thickness of the post in width and two-thirds the thickness in length. A matching mortice was cut into the upper surface of the keel near its extremity. With great care, tackles were used to hoist the stern assembly into position and lower it precisely until the tenon was seated in the mortice. Again, the assembly was shored in position so that the "false post" and inner post could be fayed in position on the forward side to function as the apron did up forward. Too, great care was taken to insure that the stern post was in precise alignment with the keel in the same manner done with the stem. Similar care was exercised to see that the transoms were truly horizontal.

The shipwrights' attention now turned to shaping and fitting the "dead wood," or rising timbers, those pieces which, collectively, increased the connection of the stem and stern posts to the keel —

further filleting to reinforce that assembly shaped like an "elbow." These great chunks of good white oak were carefully scarfed and bolted in a staggered pattern so that nowhere did scarfs align with one another.

The frigate's ribs were not single pieces of live oak, but rather assemblies of two parallel series of live oak and cedar pieces forming a "U"-shaped composite unit when assembled. The notched piece that would fit across the keel was called the "floor timber." On one side of each floor timber was attached a "cross chock," a piece of wood that eventually would play a role in attaching "first futtocks" (see below) to the keel. Directly abutting each end of the floor timber were the "second futtocks." Opposite these, were the "first futtocks." Their lower ends would rest against the sides of the keel, but not cross it, and their length was such that the butt seam between the floor timber and second futtocks occurred at about their mid-points. Above the first futtocks were the "third futtocks." All of these were of live oak. Above the second futtocks came the white oak or red cedar "top timbers," and above the third futtocks the "half top timbers." These were the principal elements of each of the ship's frames. When assembled, they were a solid two feet thick; and when all were raised in the ship, the intervals between them amounted to approximately two inches.

The frames were shaped and assembled flat on the ground using locust treenails except for the connecting floor timbers, which were put in place to drill holes for the connecting copper through bolts and then removed to the building way. Lengths of light plank ("quartering") were tacked across butt joints and a "shore" temporarily chocked in place spanning from one end of a half-frame to the other to give it support when the time came to raise it in place.

With the frames preparing, some of the floor timbers (probably every other one) were emplaced across the keel, beginning with the "main frame," the one marking the ship's greatest width, and working fore and aft from that point. Once all the flatter floor timbers were in, the "rising floors," shaping the narrowing bow and stern areas of the hull were installed. Because their deepening "vee" shapes were hard to find naturally, such pieces were assembled from several smaller ones, and so were known as "made floors." Long, pliable battens of fir or pine called "ribbands" were tacked to the floor timbers. One "ribband" passed across the heads of the floor timbers on either side, known as the "floor sirmarks," and others halfway between the heads and the keel, called the "lower sirmarks." By observing the smoothness of the curvature of these ribbands, the

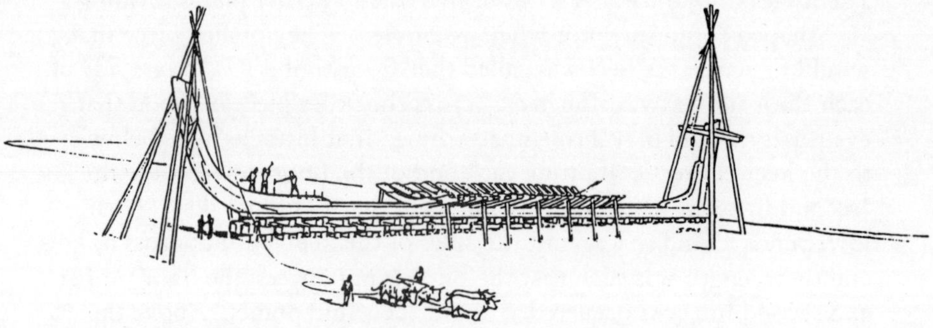

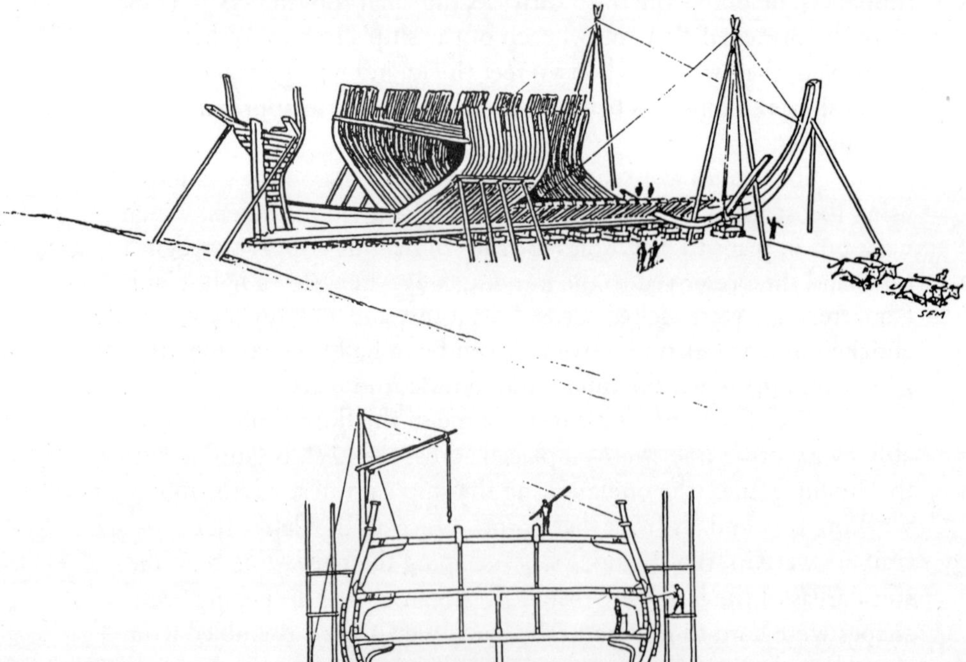

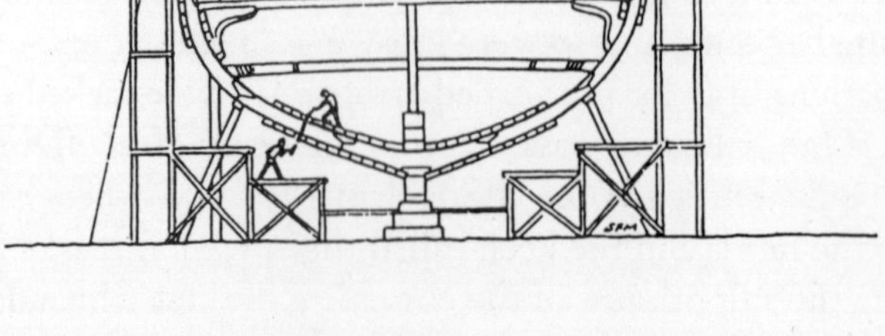

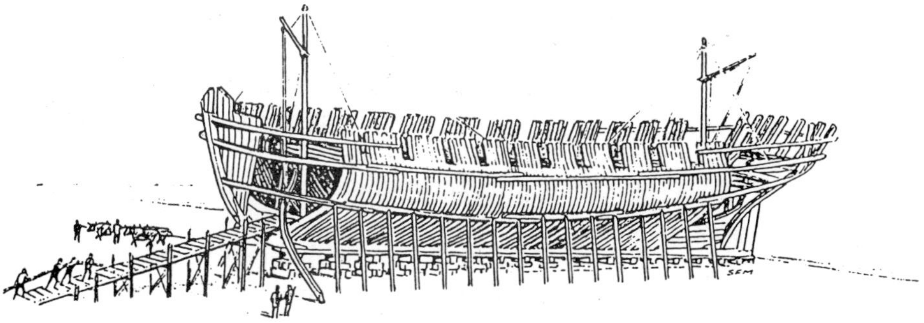

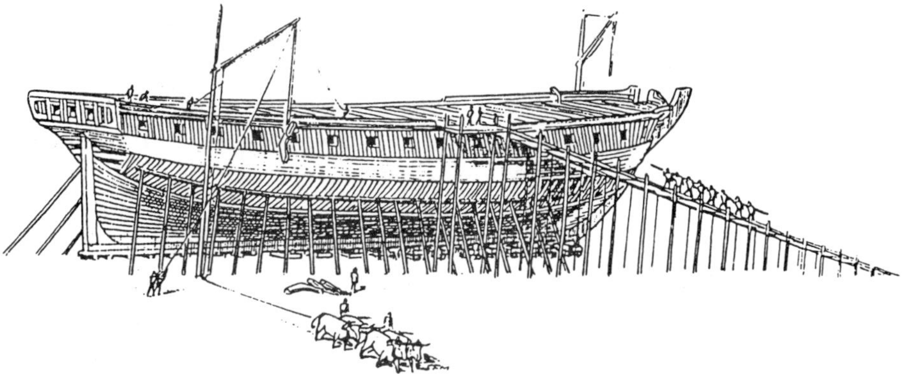

shipwrights could trim the timbers into perfect alignment and preserve the intended form of the ship. When everything was right, these floor timbers were bolted in place and the remainder fitted to conform with the structure thus formed.

The next job was to raise the "cant timbers," those "half timbers" (because they did not cross the ship's centerline) that shaped the hull between the rising floors and the hawse pieces forward, and between the rising floors and the fashion pieces aft. These elements of framework were fitted into notches ("steps") in the deadwood and at angles to the keel fore or aft, forming the rounding of the hull at the extremities.

The final task in forming the backbone was the installation of the "keelson." It was a twin to the keel, made up of pieces of white oak carefully scarfed together and trimmed to fit closely over the floor timbers where they crossed the keel. Once in place, one and three-eighth inch copper through-bolts were driven through keelson, every floor timber, and the keel, and clenched. Bolts of one-and-one-eighth inch diameter were driven through the keelson, every cross chock, and the keel and clenched. (British practice generally was to through-bolt through every other floor timber.)

Claghorn and Hartt probably were not able to follow the foregoing sequence of events exactly, for there continued to be a problem with the timely receipt of timbers from the South and of hardware items from Europe. On the 9th of September 1796, the schooner *Hannah* sailed for Boston from Philadelphia with "a lot of live oak timbers, the priority previously given to the frigate United States building in that city having resulted in an overstock." Nonetheless, building the ship continued in approximately the manner described.

When ready to begin raising the frames, a large sheave was placed on the ridge rope connecting the fore and aft sheer legs, and to it were attached several sets of tackle to be used in the process. First to be erected was the main frame, the one marking the ship's widest point. The two halves were positioned opposite one another with the butts of the second futtocks adjacent to their respective ends of the floor timber and the ends of the first futtocks in the air above the plane of the floor timbers. Hoisting both sides together so as to keep the strain as nearly equal as possible on either side of the keel, the frame halves were raised into position and shored in place. Then the process of driving in the treenails to join the several parts together was begun. Thereafter, every second or third frame was raised for and aft of the main frame position to create an "outline" of the ship before filling in all remaining frames. (All frames subsequent to the main frame were installed without their top timbers or half top timbers so that gun ports could be accounted for at the appropriate time.)

The framing of the hull was completed with the installation of the hawse pieces (containing the holes through which the anchor cables would exit the ship) between the cant timbers and the stem. At the stern, counter timbers were cut and fit to frame up the area above the transom and between the fashion pieces.

When the second session of the Fourth Congress met late that year, a naval committee was appointed in the House to look into the state of the building program and whether or not any navy was necessary. Once again headed by Federalist Josiah Parker, its first step was to ask Secretary of War (since 27 January 1796) James McHenry for a report. His response, dated 11 January 1797, said of *Constitution*:

> "The whole of the frame is raised, and is ready for planking; the wales are prepared, and it is expected will be on and fastened this month; the keelsons are now in their places and bolted off; the masts are now in hand, and the boats are building; all the dead eyes for lower and topmast shrouds are made and strapped; the knees for all the decks are procured, as well as the beams, carlings, ledges, etc; iron ballast sufficient is in store, and the necessary materials for completing the hull are procured and received.
>
> "The hemp for the cables, rigging, etc., and blocks, are in the hands of the respective tradesmen, manufacturing, and if the winter should prove favorable, there is no doubt but this frigate may be launched in July next."

In proceeding with *Constitution*'s construction, efforts were made to utilize some of the materials collected for frigates whose construction had been suspended. From Portsmouth, thirty-eight oaken knees, twenty beams, 230 oaken side and pine deck planks, and 137 miscellaneous pieces of live oak, white oak, and maple were shipped south. New York sent 126 pieces comprising 2829 cubic feet. Nonetheless, an estimate of additional sums needed to complete the trio still building included $96,571.71 for *Constitution*. This money, together with lesser amounts for *United States* and *Constellation*, was appropriated by Congress in the evening of 3 March 1797 - an hour before its term and Washington's presidency passed into history. By way of illustrating the uncertain future of the Navy on that date, no monies for manning these ships were provided, and proposals for the creation of a navy yard and a live oak preserve were defeated.

Thusfar, the necessary curved pieces of timber used in the ship's framework had come from "compass timbers," pieces formed naturally in approximately the correct curvature. For the planking, however, which required long lengths of white oak, it was necessary to force a certain amount of bending. Doing it without shattering the timber was difficult. Joshua Humphreys provided a means to render the task simpler and more certain of success:

> "It was thought prudent to contrive some method of seasoning and salting the white oak stuff, above light water, to assimilate it, as near as possible, with live oak and red cedar, in point of duration, and at the same time facilitate the bending of them on the round parts of the ships. A trunk long enough to take the longest timber in, with three large iron plates in each, at equal distance, and a simple air furnace under each plate, to boil the salt and water, which will penetrate any timber put into it, was considered the least expensive and most useful..."

Events that hitherto had been divorced from the building program were at long last coming to a head during this period and would provide the final impetus to the rebirth of an American navy. In the late spring of 1794, Washington had sent Chief Justice John Jay to England to try to put an end to the British practice of taking prize a neutral ship carrying any French property whatsoever, a course of action resorted to when the French Revolution began to spill outside national boundaries. Jay also was to settle certain questions that had caused friction since the American Revolution. He succeeded admirably.

As soon as the French learned the provisions of the Jay Treaty, Franco-American relations began a downward course. Paris saw in the treaty a shifting of American allegiance. In July 1796, the French resolved to retaliate with essentially the same policy, but practiced far more brutally by their privateers in the West Indies than by the Royal Navy. The policy was formalized by decree on 2 March 1797.

On 25 March, President John Adams, in office slightly more than three weeks, called for a special session of Congress to convene on 15 May to settle the nation's maritime problem with France. A happy circumstance occurred on 10 May when *United States* at long last was launched at the nation's capitol. Offsetting that good news was the fact that she was launched from excessively steep ways: she

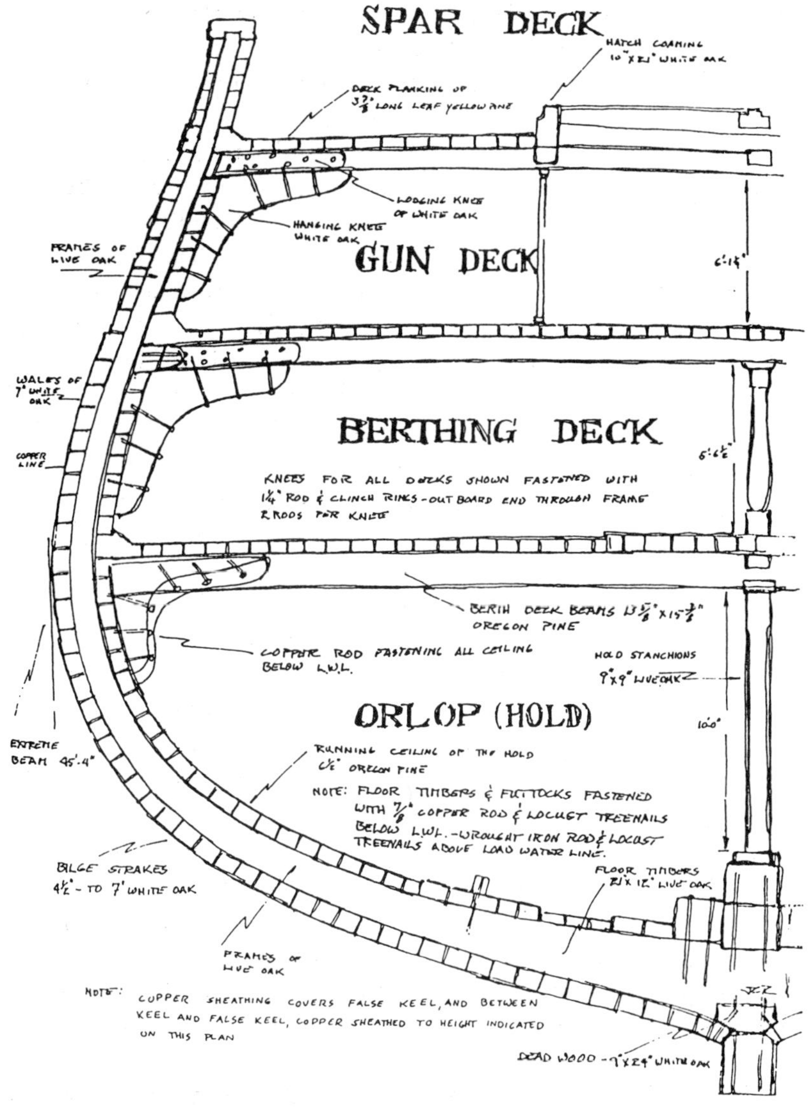
SPAR DECK
HATCH COAMING
DECK PLANKING OF
LONG LEAF YELLOW PINE
LODGING KNEE
OF WHITE OAK
HANGING KNEE
WHITE OAK
FRAMES OF
LIVE OAK
GUN DECK
6'-1½"
WALES OF
7" WHITE
OAK
COPPER
LINE
BERTHING DECK
6'-6½"
KNEES FOR ALL DECKS SHOWN FASTENED WITH
1¼" ROD & CLINCH RINGS - OUT BOARD END THROUGH FRAME
2 RODS FOR KNEE
BERTH DECK BEAMS
OREGON PINE
COPPER ROD FASTENING ALL CEILING
BELOW L.W.L.
HOLD STANCHIONS
9"x9" LIVE OAK
ORLOP (HOLD)
10'0"
EXTREME
BEAM 45'-4"
RUNNING CEILING OF THE HOLD
6½" OREGON PINE
NOTE: FLOOR TIMBERS & FUTTOCKS FASTENED
WITH ⅞" COPPER ROD & LOCUST TREENAILS
BELOW L.W.L. - WROUGHT IRON ROD & LOCUST
TREENAILS ABOVE LOAD WATER LINE.
BILGE STRAKES
4½" - TO 7" WHITE OAK
FLOOR TIMBERS
LIVE OAK
FRAMES OF
LIVE OAK
NOTE: COPPER SHEATHING COVERS FALSE KEEL, AND BETWEEN
KEEL AND FALSE KEEL, COPPER SHEATHED TO HEIGHT INDICATED
ON THIS PLAN
DEAD WOOD
WHITE OAK

shot across the river and grounded on the far bank, thereby requiring repairs even before her maiden voyage.

President Adams addressed a joint session of Congress on 16 May. He reviewed the course of events in our relations with the French and urged that some defensive measures be implemented. He recommended that the frigates be completed, that American merchant ships be convoyed, but that the building of privateers in America be banned. Clearly, it was a defensive program, one whose provisions might encourage negotiation by the French.

A greatly augmented gang of shipwrights in Boston at this time were busy preparing and installing the first planks of the ship's "skin." These were the wales, the thickest of the outer hull planks that marked the widest portion of the hull, just below where the gun deck gun ports would appear. The seven-inch thick baulks of white oak were boiled for up to seven hours in Humphreys' "trunk" to make them amenable to bending. They were then shaped and carefully pinned in place, light battens having first been used to mark out the line each should take across the frames. The lengths of these timbers varied according to the trees cut, of course, but the longest possible were used and some were more than 40 feet long. The area of the main wales was six strakes (courses of timber) high. The strakes of planking above and below the main wales gradually tapered down until the uppermost strakes were just three-and-a-half inches thick. Below the wales, the strakes thinned to four-and-a-half inches as they turned under the bilge, then thickened again to six inches at the keel. All of the strakes above the main wales had their upper surfaces mitered down so that water would not collect in the seams.

The commencement of planking marked the point at which construction speeded up markedly. Teams of shipwrights planked up and down from the wales on both sides simultaneously, while still others worked up from near the keel, and yet more on the ceiling planking inside the ship. These latter teams worked only from the keel up. Both bolts and treenails were used to fasten the planking. Bolts used above the waterline were a metal alloy in lieu of the more expensive copper ones used in the underwater body.

As the ceiling planking rose on the inner sides of the frames, other teams of shipwrights began to flesh out the internal details. The bases for the masts — the "steps" - were built astraddle the keelson. Forward, once the planking had risen sufficiently, five great "breast hooks," thirty-foot spans of curving white oak bolted through the entire thickness of the hull for reinforcement, were installed inside the bows across the stemson. Aft, smaller crotch pieces were fitted against the inner stern post.

Perhaps the most difficult task at this point was the installation of the diagonal and transom riders, those "new-fangled" stiffeners intended by Humphreys to help support the great length and bulk of his heavy frigate. They may have been shaped and lowered into the hull prior to the installation of the berth deck beams. Once the beams were in place, opposing pairs of diagonals could be jockeyed into position between the keelson and deck beams, and through-pinned. Working these great curving white oak timbers a foot or more square in cross section into place was something new and surely required the shipwrights' utmost skill.

Once the diagonals had been installed, work proceeded conventionally once again. One team installed the after orlop deck and cable tier while another placed the forward orlop. Above, berth deck planks began to go in place as the ceiling planking rose still higher. More breast hooks and crotch pieces appeared. The gun deck beams went into place, and that deck was laid. The gun deck and berth deck below were connected by three rows of stanchions. As the shipwrights moved onward and upward, other groups came in behind them: the caulkers to stuff the seams inside and out and cover the caulking with tar, and the joiners who created the pine bulkheads to form storerooms, the sickbay, and the officers' cabins.

The arguments regarding how to react to British and French attitudes toward neutral American shipping waxed hot and heavy for weeks in both houses of Congress, between Anglophile and Francophile, between Federalist and Republican. On 16 June, in the midst of this, Josiah Parker received still another report from Secretary of War McHenry concerning the frigates. Of *Constitution* he wrote:

> "The bottom of this ship is squared off, and the calkers [sic] are at work. The various decks are laying; the breasthooks, diagonal riders, and counter timbers, are all in and secured, and the mast makers are employed on the masts and yards. All the boats excepting the pinnace are built.
>
> "The riggers are at work on the rigging, which will be soon ready; the water casks are in hand; sails are preparing, and the constructor reports the ship may be launched about the twentieth of August next – the Captain is of the opinion she may be completely equipped in one month after."

As had been the case earlier, the Secretary indicated that more money would be needed – $197,636 more – for the three men-of-war. Oh yes, and pay and subsistence for their crews was now estimated at $220,938 a year.

A hot debate was fueled by this announcement of further expense, but on 1 July 1797 a bill in fourteen sections was approved. The first section authorized completion of the frigates and provided $200,000 for that purpose. Later sections dealt with manning, pay, and rations. Proposals for a navy yard and a live oak preserve again were turned down.

Building of the two frigates still on the ways now pressed forward to a conclusion. Since the Secretary's mid-June report, *Constitution*'s spar deck had gone in, the bowsprit installed, and the bulwarks around her quarterdeck completed. The final chore on her underwater body was the application in August of the copper sheathing purchased from British mills. More than 4000 sheets, each 14 by 40 inches, were tacked in place with 40 copper tacks per sheet. Three different thicknesses were employed, with the thickest going on the bows, the waterline, and the rudder. In that same month, the battery of 24-pounders was delivered from Furnace Hope. On the 5th of September, two days before *Constellation* was launched at Baltimore, *Constitution*'s anchor cable, borne by 293 men and accompanied by flags, fife and drums, was marched from Jeffrey and Russell's ropewalk into the Hartt shipyard. At long last, launching seemed imminent.

NOTES:

1. The white pine masts had been cut in the vicinity of Unity and Malta (now Windsor), Maine, by Thomas Cooper and a man named Gray, and towed to Boston by water.

2. The ten names submitted, in order, were *United States, Constitution, President, Congress, Constellation, Defender, Fortitude, Perseverance, Protector*, and *Liberty*. The President merely underlined the first five and returned the list to Pickering. (Naming the sixth unit authorized apparently was delayed because construction was not planned to begin until after John Morgan completed cutting the live oak in Georgia. The name *Chesapeake* was finally selected.) The source of the

last three names on the Pickering list can be identified, for they were among forty names sent to the Secretary by Joshua Humphreys on 20 February. His other proposed names were *Ardent, Intrepid, Formidable, Defiance, Fame, Resolution, Modeste, Prudent, Reasonable, Enterprize, Active, Robust, Thunderer, Vengeance, Terrible* (the name on the original draft for the 44s), *Invincible, Tartar, Republican, Independence, Convention, Virtuous, Justice, Senator, Representative, Negociator* [sic], *Franklin, Hancock, Lawrence, Green, Mercer, Montgomery, Putnam, Warren, Biddle, Rhode Island, Connecticut, Jersey, Delaware, Carolina,* and *Georgia*.

3. The cost of the figurehead was $719.33.

4. Sheer legs, or sheers: A pair of rough-cut mast timbers lashed together at their upper ends and set to form an inverted "V." Guyed fore and aft to hold them in position, tackles could be rigged at the apex and the assembly used as a crane. For lesser loads, it was possible to change the position of the apex by adjusting the guys to permit it to slope either way from its normal vertical position.

Part V
The Launch

For months, the burgeoning bulk of the frigate dominated the Boston waterfront just down the hill from Old North Church. The citizenry had shown considerable pride in her from the earliest days of her construction, and now that both *United States* and *Constellation* had been launched, they were most anxious that "their" ship likewise be afloat. The two major newspapers discussed her design and building progress according to their political preference: the Federalist *Columbian Centinel* waxed poetic about her form and strength; the Republican Chronicle assailed Federalist bungling and sloth in the pace of construction.

A ship, when ready to launch, is not a finished product — nor was it in 1797. The hull, with its outer and ceiling planking, was complete, caulked, and coppered. Figurehead and other decorations were in place. All of the internal compartmentation probably was not complete. Virtually none of her furnishings — capstans, most anchors, guns — were aboard. No masts had been stepped nor rigging rigged. Even so, the 1500 or so trees employed in bringing the embryonic frigate, as she was designated, to her present state had contributed more than 1200 tons to her hefty bulk. And there she sat in late August, her Hercules figurehead looming up above Ship Street (Commercial Street today) as she awaited the final preparations for the big day.

The first step in the countdown was to install the bilge ways or launching ways. These consisted of two stout wooden rails laid on the slip bed parallel to the ship's centerline and about ten feet out on either side of it. Each was about two-and-a-half feet broad, securely spiked to the groundway. Additionally, each was shored all along its length to prevent spread when the ship's weight came on it.

Crucial to the laying of the bilge ways was their slope, or declivity. If it was insufficient, it would be difficult to get the hull moving. If it did move, the longer period of movement greatly raised the danger that the stresses would overcome the relatively light launching cradle and cause the ship to fall off either side — most probably a total loss. Or, again because of the slow motion, cause the forefoot to take excessive strain for too long as the water buoyed the stern up off the ways. thereby twisting the ship's structure, or perhaps even breaking her back. Too great a slope on the other hand would result in a high-speed water entry and danger to the ship through collision or grounding. Sailors are suspicious of ships with such inauspicious beginnings. According to one authority writing at the turn of the 19th Century, a declivity of 5/8 of an inch per foot — about 5% — was an adequate amount.

After laying the bilge ways, the Constructor then set about erecting the cradles, fore and aft. But first, he liberally coated the bilge ways with a mix of soap and tallow. Then, two thick planks of fir were placed atop the ways, their undersides having been similarly lubricated. Large, curved pieces called "spurs," exactly fitting the outside shape of the hull, then were fixed in place on the planks and forelocked through the hull with three bolts. Typically, there would have been four spurs cradling the bow and five near the stern. Braces were fitted between the base planks of the cradles and the ship's keel to increase the structure's rigidity.

Beneath the stem and between the bilgeways was installed the driver screw, a simple if over-large jack with one of its sides against a transverse member of the ground way and the other against the ship's stem. Two screws connected the sides and kept them apart with just sufficient pressure to hold its position between the ship and the way. Further to assist in getting the ship started down the ways, powerful tackles were rigged from the forward part of the cradle on each side to bollards set alongside the ship near the stern and shore line.

Finally, to prevent the ship from launching itself prematurely, long baulks of timber, each with the forward portion hinged, were affixed to the outer sides of the launch ways below the forward cradle. The forward ends were seated against blocks of wood attached to the forward part of the cradle and held in place by wedges with ropes attached. When the "big moment" came, the wedges would be drawn and the hinged portions dropped, clearing the way for the ship to begin her shortest, perhaps most dangerous, journey.

After having accomplished all this work preparatory to launching, came the time to fit a final member onto the ship's underwater body: the false keel. Composed of a number of pieces of six- or eight-inch thick timber, it was inserted in stages, stapled to the keel on each side, and scarphed to form a unified whole as the shipwrights sequentially removed the splitting blocks. With the splitting blocks gone, the ship's total weight was removed from the groundways and rested on the launching cradle. It needed only a suitably high tide and the assemblage of dignitaries and spectators for her launch.

As mentioned earlier, the launch of *USS United States* on 10 May had gone awry and she had been damaged in the process. This resulted in Secretary of War James McHenry sending letters to Baltimore and Boston warning builders there that he desired the vessels "should be launched in the safest manner and with as little expence to the United States as possible." The launch of *USS Constellation* on 7 September was preceded by a painstaking inspection of the ways and review of procedures; it went off without a hitch.

On 10 September, Secretary McHenry responded to a six-day-old letter from Boston Constructor George Claghorn suggesting the ship be launched in the present month by "noticing...that the work which must be done after getting her into the water could be cheapest performed while on the stocks. If in your opinion it would be unsafe to trust the tides in October I very readily agree to her being launched in this month: but if we may venture the delay until October and it would be a saving in point of expense, I should prefer that, especially as it does not appear to me that any thing could be gained by a premature launch."

Claghorn's response to this letter is not on record, so his reaction to it is unknown. It is known, however, that the citizens of Boston were eager to see the big frigate afloat. It may have been this local pressure that caused Claghorn, in the absence of any cautionary consultative visit from Joshua Humphreys, to ignore the Secretary's view and set 20 September as the big day.

The two major city newspapers discussed her design and building progress according to their political preference. A few days before the scheduled launch, the Federalist *Columbian Centinel* published an extensive appreciation of the ship:

> "A correspondent who lately took a critical view of the new frigate, was struck, he says, by the analogy between the ship and her name, viz., the '*Constitution*.' First, her timbers are of our own growth, sound and excellent, and put together

judiciously and faithfully. There is no sawdust and putty crammed in to fill up flaws and cracks and hide imperfect joints: but all is firm, solid, and connected like the oak tree with its branches.

"Secondly, her figure or general outline is, like the *Constitution*, beautiful: and she carries at her head the figure of Hercules, with his club and lion's skin, and everybody knows that by the allegory of Hercules is meant heroic virtue.

"Thirdly, the most important part of her, as regards the safety of the people and which is immersed in a treacherous element, is covered with copper to secure her against those small but destructive vermin who like our Jacobins, work out of sight, secretly and insidiously, in boring holes to let in the destroying element and sink the ship.

"Fourthly, she, like the *Constitution*, is built for the safety of the people, and their property: and carries the ensigns of our national honor, with the means of defending it.

"Fifthly, like the *Constitution* she will be conducted by citizens of different ranks and powers, as to command and order, but all conspiring to form a harmonious whole.

"Sixthly, she will be commanded by officers whom we can trust and support. "Seventhly, she will launch forth into that element which connects the world together, as the *Constitution* did the political one, amidst the shouts and acclamations of the people whose voice created her. That Heaven may long preserve both the original and the type is the hearty prayer of all — save Jacobins and worms."

The Jeffersonian Democrats — the "Jacobins" noted a moment ago — responded in kind in the *Chronicle*. They'll have their turn in a moment.

Many were the preparations made for the long-awaited event. President John Adams and his suite were invited, as were the Governor of the Commonwealth, Increase Summer, and Boston's selectmen. Enterprising nearby property owners and boatmen sought to capitalize on the occasion by erecting viewing platforms for paying customers on the one hand and hiring out their boats to well-heeled rubberneckers on the other. People even were expected to gather on Noddle's Island across the way to see the mighty *Constitution* "launch forth into that element which connects the world together." In town, dinners, dances, and dramatics would celebrate the occasion.

Constructor George Claghorn took note of this growing

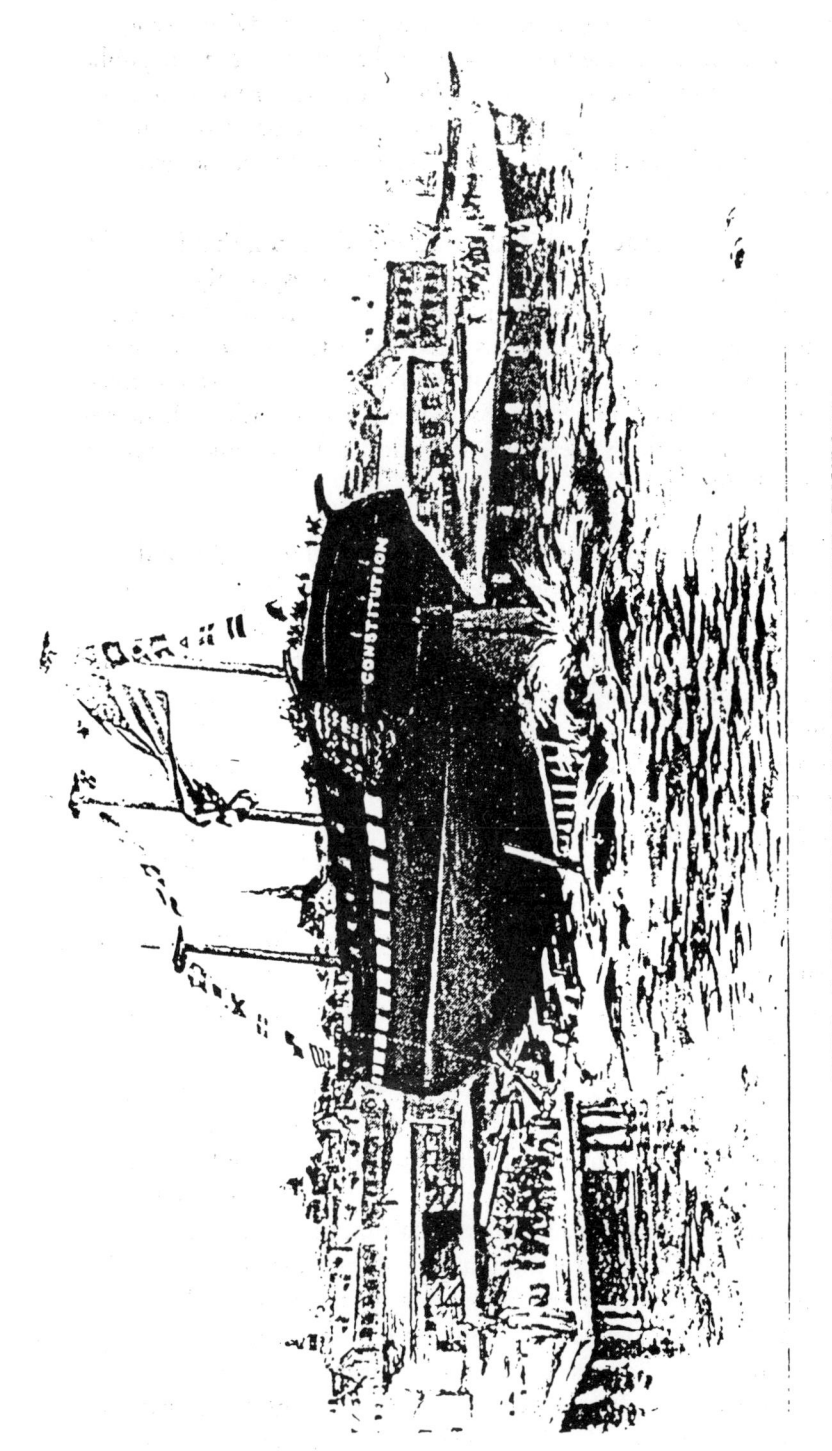

THE LAUNCHING OF THE CONSTITUTION

enthusiasm and published a circular on 18 September advising that, because of the limited space in the Hartt yard and a concern for public safety, only the President, Governor, Lieutenant Governor, and their respective suites, and the invited select few would be permitted "inside the fence" to watch the spectacle. Claghorn's concern was so great that he wrote:

> "It is suggested that as the tide would be full, that it would be necessary to the safety of the spectators, especially women and children, that they do not approach in crowds, too near the margin of the contiguous wharves, as the sudden entrance of so large a body as the frigate will occasion an instantaneous swell of water, the height of which cannot be easily calculated, and against which therefore, discretion of the people ought amply to guard."

The 20th of September 1797 dawned cold, but bright, and altogether a pleasant day. Thousands thronged from Boston and the nearby countryside to take every possible perch from which the launching could be observed. At 11:20 A. M., the calculated moment of high tide, Colonel Claghorn gave the order to knock out the blocks and a hush fell over the crowd as it gathered itself to cheer the frigate's first moments afloat. Soon, all the blocks were gone - but the ship failed to move. A mortified Claghorn ordered the use of screws to get her going, and she began to move. After twenty-seven feet, she would move no farther. A portion of the ways had settled half an inch, and left her stuck. The blocks and shores were replaced, and the disappointed thousands went home. *Constitution*'s first moment in the sun had been a fizzle. Predictably, the *Centinel* commiserated with Claghorn. The Republican *Chronicle* — "that speaking trumpet of the devil" — gleefully let fly:

> "'The Launch.' That was to be. A full account of yesterday's frolick at the Navy Yard, we presume, will be gratifying to all parties as perhaps anything we could publish...
>
> "After the President, his suite and the ladies got well seated in their respective places of destination...the operation of launching the frigate commenced. Block after block fell and the main supports were quickly leveled to the ground. At length the frigate was left to her own destination. But alas! she paused! She reflected on the propriety of entering her 'destined element.' She seemed to hesitate whether it was for the interest of the United States to take her station on the

principles she was fabricated.

"During the consultation of the timbers which composed her, a large body of some of those (falsely styled Federalists) applied their strength to 'the long pull, the pull together,' and with the assistance of screws they gave the frigate '*Constitution*' a start equal to what the same party gave the federal *Constitution* in the adoption of the British treaty.

"On board the frigate we observed the 'Centinel' Major [Russell, the publisher of the other newspaper] who has already anticipated in his paper its full egress into the water but as he observes 'that it will launch forth into that element which connects the world together, as the *Constitution* did the political one' we are apt to conclude, from the event, that he is an anti-Federalist: for we would not suppose the Federal Constitution was screwed into the people; that it was impeded in its progress, for want of system in its arrangement; and that, finally, by mere dint of manoeuvering, it was adopted by the citizens."

Mishap notwithstanding, the Haymarket Theatre presented a musical play by John Hodgkinson entitled "The Launch, or Huzza for the *Constitution*," that evening. It is said to have been a box office success.

Let the press have their fun. The next day, after taking measurements and laying his plans carefully, Claghorn wedged the ship up two inches in a fifty-minute operation, and set about correcting the defects in the ways as he saw them. By evening, all again appeared to be in readiness.

On 22 September, with almost no-one the wiser, the launch sequence again was started. This time the ship moved thirty-one feet and was about to enter the water when she stopped abruptly. Claghorn was sorely tempted to try and force her on in, but he recognized the real possibility of her becoming hung up, half in and half out, and wisely desisted. The settling of another portion of the ways, this time by one and five-eighths inches, had frustrated the plan.

This second miscarriage only served to heighten the verbal storm between Federalists and Democrats. And among seafaring folk there were those who were wagging their heads knowingly and declaring that the vessel was an "unlucky ship."

Claghorn reported his two failures to Secretary McHenry in a letter dated 24 September. Of the situation he wrote:

"I had formed the inclined plane upon the smallest angle

that I conceived would convey the ship into the water, in order that she might make her plunge with the least violence, and thereby prevent any strain or injury; I must give the ways more descent, which will remedy the defect occasioned by the settling of the new wharf; and I am fully confident that the next trial, at the high tides in October, will be attended with success; in the mean time I shall proceed in completing the ship on the stocks."

Poor Claghorn! How the chickens had come home to roost! He had been cautious in constructing the launching ways in order that the ship not be launched precipitately; and he had been precipitate in pressing a September launch contrary to the Secretary's expressed preference. While McHenry seems not to have taunted the poor man, the same could not be said of his fellow Bostonians. Wrote Rachel Bradford of Boston to Elias Boudinot at Philadelphia on 26 September:

"I suppose you have seen in the papers...an account of the disappointment we have all had in the launching of the Frigate... The Jacobins have greatly exulted and the Chronicle their organ of impudent speeches has dealt out many sad predictions, and sarcastic remarks, on the failure of the attempt to launch her whilst all the force of Benevolence, and the aids of good natural wit on the part of the opposite party have appeared thro' the Mercury to give a handsom [sic] coulering [sic] to the business and sooth [sic] the Chagrine [sic] of the Master Ship Builder who actually appeared to have lost flesh in eight and forty hours, from mortification..."

21 October 1797 was a cold, overcast day. An east wind swept across the Hartt yard. Early that morning, George Claghorn caused one of *Constitution*'s 24-pounder cannon, which were not yet on board, to be fired as an announcement to anyone interested that he was ready to try again at high tide. By noon "a very numerous and brilliant collection of citizens assembled at the spectacle." Among those on board for the occasion were Captain Samuel Nicholson, prickly as a porcupine and eager to have sole authority over the frigate; Captain James Sever, visiting from his post in Portsmouth, New Hampshire; Mr. George Ticknor; Mr. Benjamin Russell (of the *Columbian Centinel*) and his guests, the Duc de Chartres (later King Louis Philippe of France), the Duc de Montpensier, Comte de Beaujolais, and Prince Tallyrand, together with a number of ladies. A few moments later, Claghorn gave the order to knock out the blocks

and shores, and this time the large frigate moved promptly and swiftly into the harbor waters. As she went, Captain Sever broke a bottle of Madeira on the heel of her bowsprit, declaring her to be named "*Constitution*."[1]

Once anchored, the yard was signaled and *Constitution*'s cannon on shore "announced to the neighboring country that *CONSTITUTION* WAS SECURE." Reported the *Centinel*:

> "Such was the regular obliquity of the ways, that she came to anchor within 200 yards of them, without the least strain or meeting or causing the most trifling accident. And now she rides at her mooring in the harbor, a pleasing sight, to those who contemplate her as the germ of a naval force, which in no remote period of time will protect the flag of the United States from the depredations of piratical marauders."

Even the usually derisive *Chronicle* could not resist waxing romantically eloquent when it reported that "she moved with a most graceful dignity into the embraces of the surrounding waters;...this child of the ocean was safely delivered in the cradle, to the protection of Neptune to be suckled at the breast of 'fair Bellona.'"

For all the satisfaction he must have felt that day, Captain Nicholson was frustrated in the exercise of what he considered to be one of his prerogatives: the breaking of the Stars and Stripes aboard the new ship. Two shipyard workers, Samuel Bently and a man named Harris, in return for the many occasions when Nicholson had vented his spleen on the work force, slipped aboard while the Captain was at a post-launch dinner ashore, and hoisted the colors. Nicholson, of course, was furious when he returned and found that he had been preempted. But the flag remained, fluttering in the damp, chill air.

NOTE:

1. The time of launching is variously reported as "fifteen minutes before meridian, "fifteen minutes after twelve," and "12:30." High tide in that part of Boston Harbor on that date was at about 1208. While Captain Sever is most frequently reported as having christened the ship, at least one source stated that Captain Nicholson did it himself. In any event, *Constitution*'s christening is the earliest recorded in the United States Navy. It is said that the bottle of Madeira came from the cellar of the Honorable Thomas Russell.

Part VI
Completion & Cost

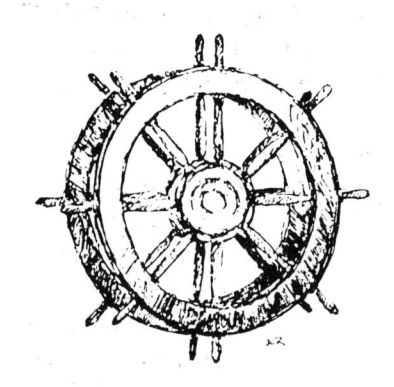

At the time *Constitution* was launched, there was an atmosphere of watchful waiting in Philadelphia. Our free trade upon the high seas was being affected by the belligerents in Europe, Britain and France – principally the latter. Barbary pirates were relegated to secondary concern for the time being. The country seemed ready to take some defensive measures, but hoped the situation could be resolved without bloodshed.

President Adams addressed the second session of the Fifth Congress as it convened late in November, noting that commerce was essential to this country and that it was wise to make preparations to defend that commerce in a timely manner. These defenses, he said, should be only so much as can be provided by taxes – no reliance should be placed on loans – a position with which both houses of the Congress agreed.

As the talks drifted along in Paris, so, too, did governmental efforts at defense preparations. By late December, the frigate at Boston had virtually all her joiner work completed (the installation of interior bulkheads, etc.), all the lower masts had been stepped, and were being rigged. In January 1798, Congress once again was investigating the cost of the frigates and Secretary McHenry's request for a deficiency appropriation of $396,212 to get on with that program and other naval matters. In the absence of funds, completion and outfitting proceeded slowly.

On 5 March, President Adams relayed to Congress a letter he had received from his emissaries in France which said, in part, "We can only repeat there exists no hope...that the objects of our mission will be in any way accomplished." As a result, defense legislation began to move. The Federalists and Republicans spent two weeks in attacking one another's honor and exchanging vituperations before finally appropriating the requested monies. When the famous "XYZ" papers, delineating French diplomatic machinations, were passed to the Congress on 2 April, money ceased, for the time being, to be a serious problem to the embryonic navy.

During the month of March, Colonel Claghorn had received from the Naval Store six 8.25-inch howitzers for *Constitution*. These, it will be recalled, had been cast by Paul Revere nearly three years earlier in accordance with the original plan to equip each ship with a combination of 24- and 12-pounder long guns and these howitzers. Claghorn's ship, however, contrary to the ships of Humphreys design, was completed with bulwarks enclosing the entire quarterdeck in lieu of the open railing depicted in the drawings provided from Philadelphia. The next two months were spent trying to find a way to mount these weapons compatibly with the bulwarks. Defeat finally was admitted to the Secretary in May; the howitzers appear to have spent the next two years in her hold as a part of the ballast.

Secretary McHenry, on 9 April, directed Intendent of Military Stores Samuel Hodgdon to have "transported to the Frigate *Constitution* at Boston in the safest and most expeditious manner" a long list of materials including 100 pairs of pistols, 100 boarding axes, 200 cutlasses, 2957 24-pounder shot, 750 stools of 24-pounder grape and cannister, 450 24-pounder double-headed and chain shot, 60 muskets (for Marines), 3000 flannel cartridges for 24-pounders, and a host of other weapons-related items. A 242-pound bell was provided by Paul Revere for $108.90. On the 21st, McHenry informed Captain Nicholson that "The Medecine Chest...and a complete Sett [sic] of instruments...will be sent as soon as possible." He also approved of Nicholson's proposal to have Paul Revere cast "Canonades" for the ship, subject to "the usual Proofs and Examinations." This same letter directed Nicholson to select "proper Characters for Boatswain, Gunner, Carpenter, Sailmaker, and Midship-Men."

With the need apparent and the way now cleared for a Navy in fact, Congress acted to end the War Department's stewardship of the new force. Events set afoot by the President's announcement on 5 March of French persiflage resulted, on 27 April, in a bill authorizing expansion of the Navy by not more than twelve vessels carrying no more than twenty-two guns each, and on 30 April in the establishment of a Department of the Navy in the executive branch of the

TRANSPARENT VIEW OF BOW

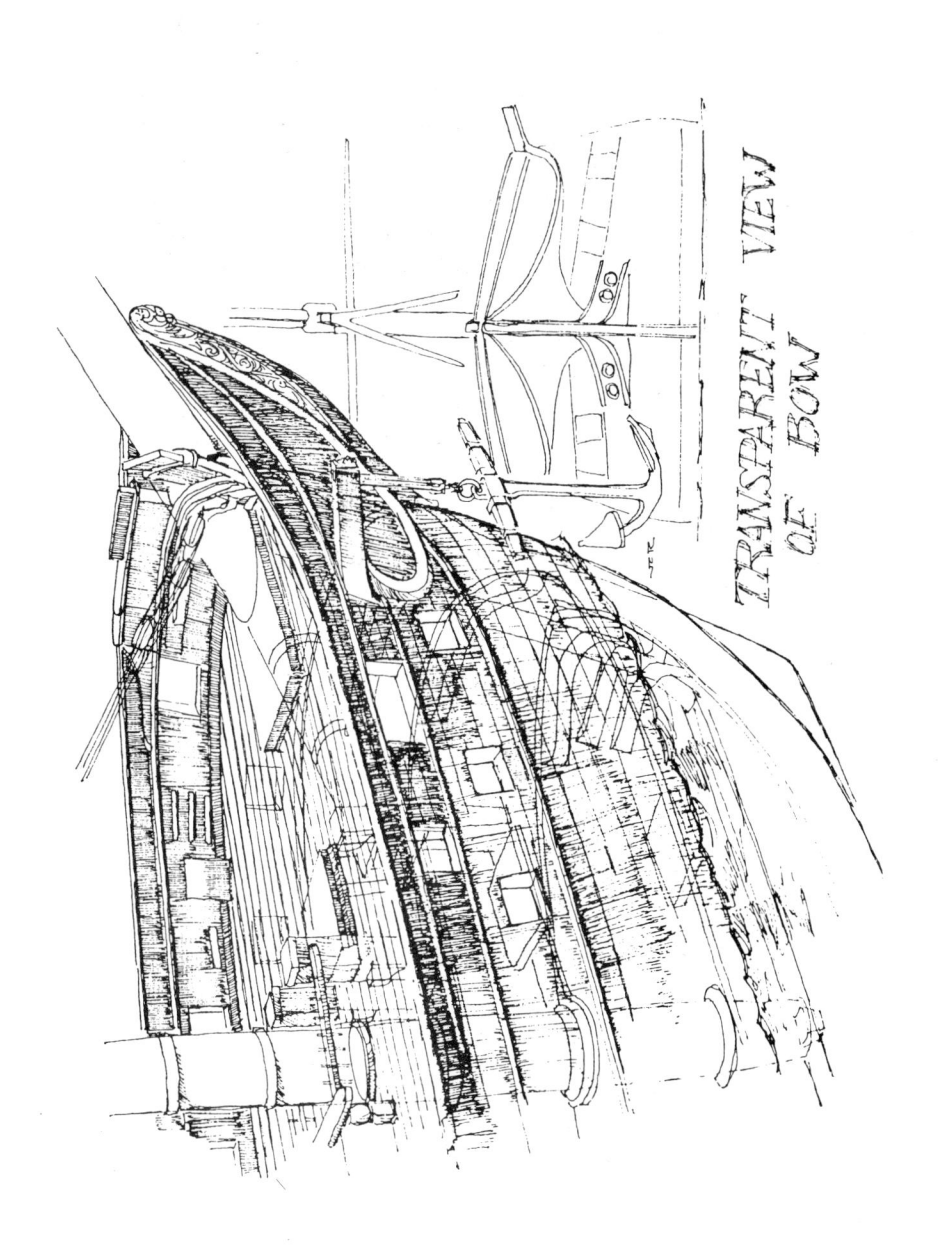

government. George Cabot of Massachusetts was nominated by the President to be the first Secretary of the Navy on 1 May and confirmed by the Senate two days later; on 11 May, Cabot declined to serve because he felt unqualified. On second try, Adams nominated Benjamin Stoddert of Georgetown, Maryland, who also was confirmed, who accepted, and whose first day in office was 18 June.

Meanwhile, *Constitution*'s outfitting went on. Midshipman James McDonough was, on 4 May, ordered to report "forthwith and without Loss of Time." The next day, Captain Nicholson was directed "to repair on board...and to lose no time in completing, equipping, and manning her for Sea." He was to "open houses of Rendezvous in proper Places" and engage 150 able seamen and 103 midshipmen and ordinary seamen "all certified healthy by the Surgeon, for twelve Months unless sooner discharged."

Lieutenant Lemuel Clark received his orders on 5 May, as well, as the officer in charge of *Constitution*'s Marine detachment. The directive he received from the War Department concerning Marine recruitment stated:

> "No Negro, Mulatto or Indian to be enlisted nor any Description of Men except Natives of fair Conduct or Foreigners of unequivocal Characters for Sobriety and Fidelity."

This prohibition was directed to the Marine officer in charge on each frigate, but was not a part of the guidance relative to sailor recruitment.

Captain Nicholson lost no time in recruiting his crew. In the *Columbian Centinel* there appeared this advertisement dated 12 May:

"Frigate CONSTITUTION

"To all able-bodied and patriotic Seamen, who are willing to serve their Country, and Support its Cause:

"The President of the United States, having ordered Captain and Commander of the good Frigate *CONSTITUTION*, of 44 guns, now riding in the harbor of Boston, to employ the most vigorous exertions to put said ship, as speedily as possible, in a situation to sail at the shortest command.

"Notice is hereby given, That a HOUSE OF RENDEZVOUS is opened at the sign of the Federal Eagle, kept by Mrs. BROADERS, in Fore-street; - where ONE HUNDRED and FIFTY able Seamen, and NINETY FIVE ordinary Seamen, will have an opportunity of entering into the service of their country for One Year, unless sooner discharged by the President of the United States. To all able bodied Seamen, the sum of SEVENTEEN DOLLARS; and to all ORDINARY SEAMEN the sum of TEN DOLLARS per month, will be given; and two months advance will be paid by the Recruiting Officer, if necessary.

"None will be allowed to enter this honorable service, but such as are well organized, healthy and robust; and free from scorbutic and consumptive affections.

"A glorious opportunity now presents to the brave and hardy Seamen of New-England, to enter the service of their country - to avenge its wrongs - and to protect its rights on the ocean. Those brave Lads, are now invited to repair to the FLAGG [sic] of the *CONSTITUTION* now flying at the above rendezvous; where they shall be kindly received, handsomely entertained, and may enter into immediate pay.

"Samuel NICHOLSON

"Commander United States Frigate *CONSTITUTION*

"At the above rendezvous Lt. Clarke of the Marines, will enlist three Sargeants [sic], three Corporals, one Armourer, one Drummer, one Fifer, and fifty privates to compose a company for the Ship *CONSTITUTION*. None can be inlisted [sic] who are not five feet, six inches high."

On the morning of 15 May, 17-year-old William Bryant, of Ipswich, Massachusetts, signed on and that afternoon "was in the boat with the first recruits that ever went on board of that ship...no officers on board at that time but petty officers."

Throughout May, as recruiting went on, stores were arriving in ever greater quantities for the ship: 1792 pounds of musket and pistol balls, two bales of bunting, 1755 gallons of brandy, forty-eight capstan bars, chaldrons of sea coal, thirty 24-pounder cannon, a grindstone, over 500 handspikes, ninety lanterns, 2143 gallons of rum, six speaking trumpets, a chest of carpenter tools - the variety and numbers of items necessary to the small, seagoing community was staggering to the imagination.

Congress finally agreed on "An Act More Effectually to Protect the Commerce and Coasts of the United States" on 28 May. Not indicated in the title was the fact that it was directed solely at "armed vessels sailing under authority or pretense of authority from the Republic of France." Some Congressmen had hoped Great Britain would be included, but there was insufficient support for it. President

TRANSPARENT VIEW OF STERN

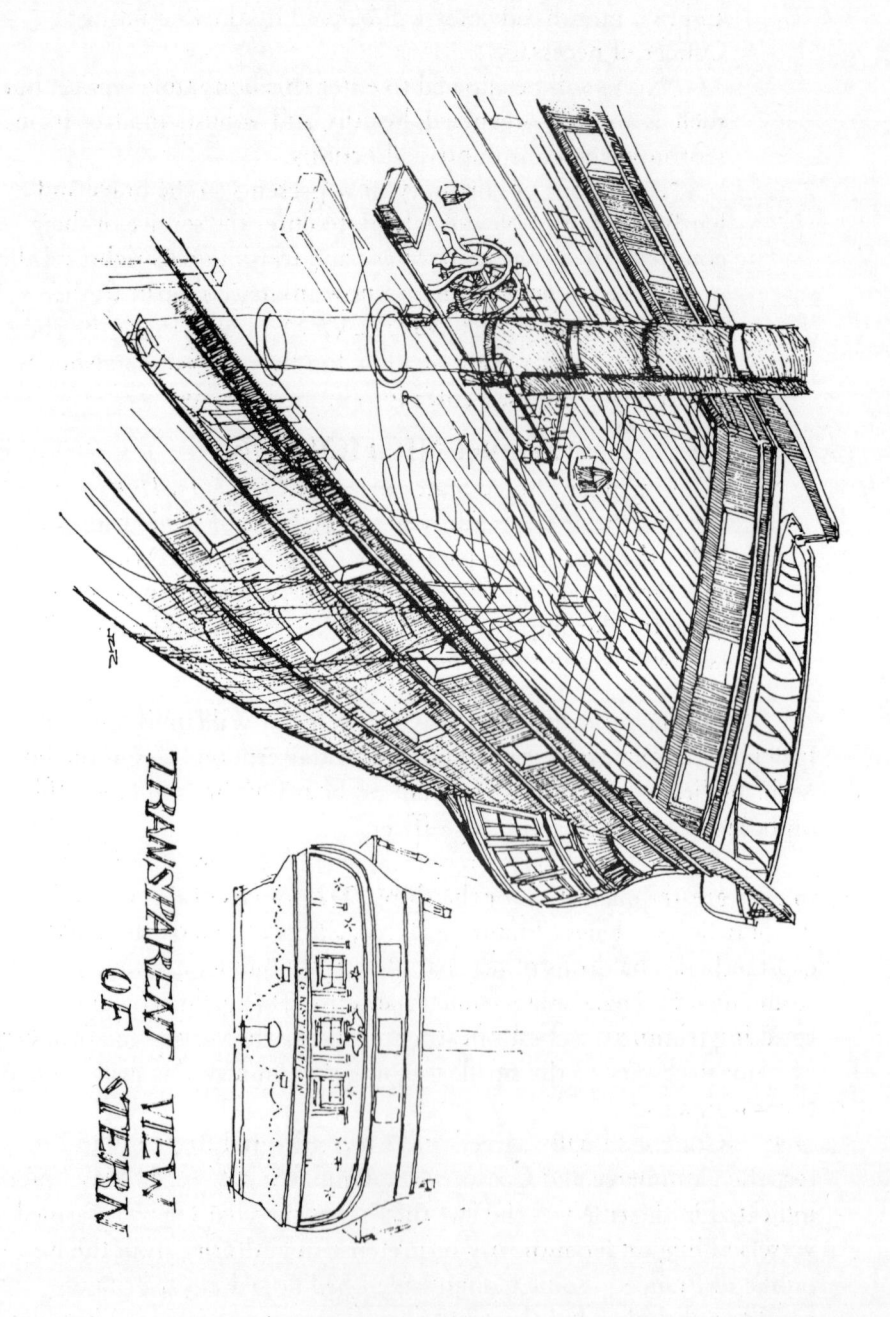

Adams issued his instructions to the Navy the very same day, for his captains "to seize take and bring into any Port of the United States... any Armed Vessels sailing under Authority... from France" off our coasts attacking, or waiting to attack, our merchantmen. Those taken by the French were to be recaptured when encountered. The orders were rushed to the Delaware Capes, where the sloop of war *Ganges*, a con-verted merchantman carrying 26 guns under the command of Captain Richard Dale (John Paul Jones' First Lieutenant in *Bon Homme Richard* during the Revolution), was waiting eagerly to be first out.

Congressional action made it imperative that the Navy, for which so many had striven so long, get in action as soon as possible to demonstrate its worth. The Secretary of War, in the absence of the new Secretary of the Navy, took positive steps to overcome equipment and supply deficiencies. When Captain Nicholson reported that he was having problems mounting the howitzers behind the quarterdeck bulwarks, Knox directed that they be landed rather than cut larger gun ports. About two weeks later, on 30 May, he took the unusual step of writing to the Governor of Massachusetts for help. Noting the "failure of a Contract" for 12-pounders, he requested that fourteen or sixteen of the nineteen iron 18-pounders the Commonwealth had on Castle Island be loaned to the Federal Government, together with a quantity of shot. (Nicholson had inspected the guns and had suggested this course of action.) The loan was to terminate when the correct guns were available for the frigate. The Governor agreed. In the meantime, however, someone located some 12-pounders and got them to the ship. *Who* is a mystery, as is the source. The upshot of all this activity was that, by mid-June, *Constitution* had been armed with thirty 24-pounders from Furnace Hope, the sixteen borrowed 18-pounders, *and* the fourteen windfall 12-pounders. No howitzers.[1]

Captain Nicholson had a reputation for being a tough, abrasive character who often acted before having all the facts pertinent to the action in hand. There is extant a letter from Stephen Higginson, General Jackson's successor as Naval Agent in Boston, presumably to the Secretary of War, that sheds contemporary light on *Constitution*'s first Commanding Officer and some of his subordinate officers during this outfitting period:

> "Dear Sir...it is both unpleasant & injurious to have popular clamours at the appointments & other measures of Government, especially when it is the general opinion that

the complaints are well founded... Capt. N: is in my estimation a rough blustering Tar merely, he is a good seaman probably & is no doubt acquainted with many or most parts of his duty, So far as it relates to practical seamanship; but he wants points much more important as a Commander in my view, prudence, judgment & reflection are no traits in his character, nor will he ever improve. [H]is noise & vanity is disgusting to the Sailors; but a belief that he wants courage goes much further to render him unpopular with them... Mr Cordis the second Lt. is a young man, who possesses none of the requisites, he is deficient in every point, essential to a good Officer, he is said to be intemperate & he looks like it. — the Surgeon, Read, is the opposite of what he ought to be in Morals, in politics & in his profession. There is not a man in this town who would trust the life of a dog in his hands. [H]is second, Blake, is...the same, but not so highly finished..."

Higginson got a reply to his assessment, dated 7 June, to which he responded on the 12th. Expanding on the theme his earlier letter he wrote:

"...the Ship has not Officers to give her a fair chance if She can be got to Sea... Capt. N: is not intemperate... [H]is defects are more natural than acquired, they consist in want of natural talents rather than vicious habits; he is neither a Gentleman, nor a popular man with the Sailors...but I know of no criminal conduct or neglect...as would justify perhaps a dismissal from office... I believe that the characters I sketched to you in a former Letter will give a correct view of the Officers of the Frigate here... I should tremble for the issue should she meet a french [sic] Cruiser of equal force, though I am sure we have a great national superiority over them for naval operations."

The Naval Agent received a second letter, dated 11 June, which indicated that almost 200 men had been shipped "in the out posts," and offered the hope that "Mr. Beale [sic] who is appointed 3rd Lt. is a smart young man, & will be a good officer ... and ... will animate the rest, and give some efficiency."

Constellation began her first cruise the last week in June. *United States* was out early in July. Because of Nicholson's unpopularity, and because those Bostonians so patriotically inclined had the option of enlisting with Captain Sever in the 18-gun ship *Herald*, *Constitution* remained in port. On 2 July, Nicholson managed to set a few

The Anchor Detail

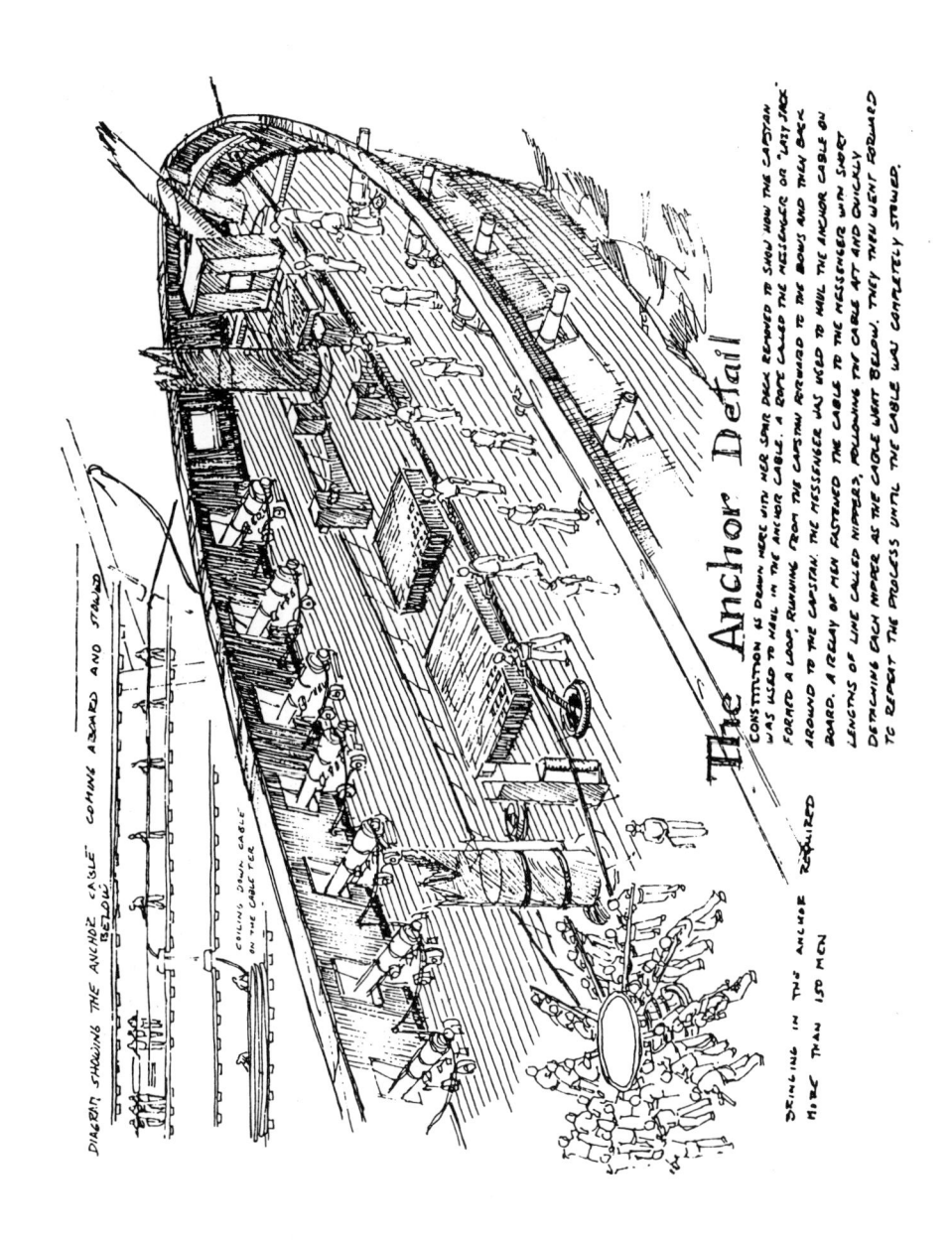

Constitution is drawn here with her spar deck removed to show how the capstan was used to haul in the anchor cable. A rope called the messenger or "lazy jack" formed a loop, running from the capstan forward to the bows and then back around to the capstan. The messenger was used to haul the anchor cable on board. A relay of men fastened the cable to the messenger with short lengths of line called nippers, following the cable aft and quickly detaching each nipper as the cable went below. They then went forward to repeat the process until the cable was completely stowed.

Diagram showing the anchor cable coming aboard and stowed below

Coiling down cable in the cable tier

Bringing in the anchor required more than 150 men

sail for the first time, and moved the ship out to King's (now President's) Roads, from whence his crew would be less likely to attempt desertion, and where he completed loading powder and shot from Castle Island, and provisions from the city.

Secretary of the Navy Benjamin Stoddert's first written comment concerning the frigate was made to Higginson on 5 July: "I wish I knew the exact situation of the frigate *Constitution*." The next day, Nicholson reported to him:

> "...we regularly make two loads a day in the long boat from the Island... Our Carpenters are mounting the Carronades in the Tops, and slinging the lower yards with chain... The Gunner with 5 of his Crew are gone to the Castle, filling cartridges... [W]e are now covering the lead in the bread room with thin boards, after which I will take the bread and Sails, likewise the powder on board —"

On 12 July 1798, Stoddert sent Nicholson his orders. They were to patrol off the coast "to secure from the Depradations [sic] of the French Cruisers, the principal Ports of New Hampshire, Massachusetts, & Rhode Island, & to pay some attention to that of New York." He was authorized to capture French armed vessels anywhere on the high seas, as well as in territorial waters. Captain Dale in *Ganges* had the next patrol south, from Long Island to Cape Henry. Nicholson was to check at Newport, Rhode Island, at 10-12 day intervals to receive any later communications. Detailed instructions relative to prizes and relations with ships of other than French registry were included.

Constitution finally was ready for sea on 22 July 1798. It was not an auspicious beginning. Evidence was strong that she was jinxed: it had taken three tries to launch her. Her Captain had an abysmal reputation, and the officers were, in the main, drunks and libertines - and probably professionally second-rate, to boot. The crew was unhappy and demoralized. Only the bright, breezy weather augured well for this, the newest warship of the young United States.

TALLYING UP THE BILL

Constitution's gestation period had lasted for more than four years. In the appropriation providing initial monies for her construction, approximately $115,000 had been provided. When all was said

Rigging out the Studding Sails

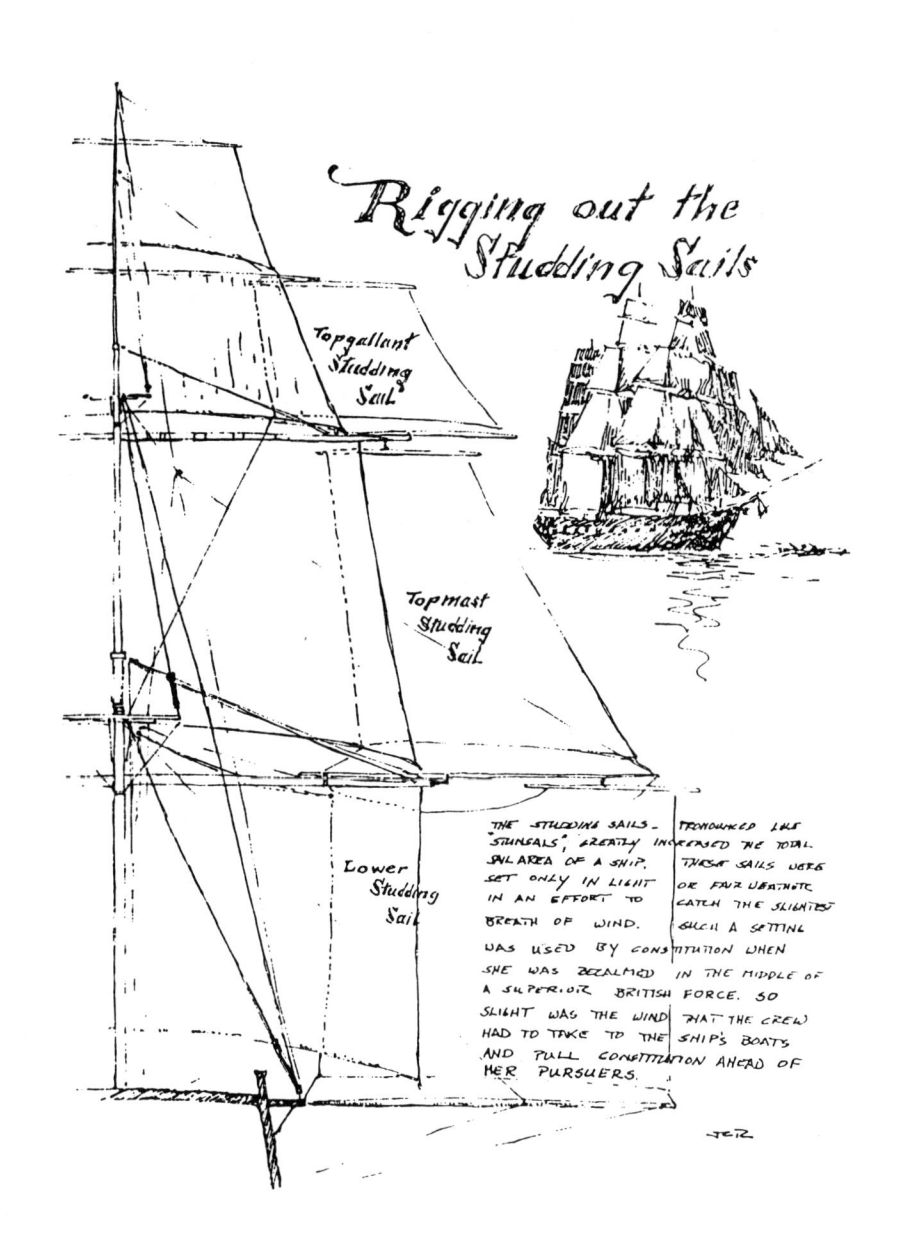

Topgallant Studding Sail

Topmast Studding Sail

Lower Studding Sail

The studding sails — pronounced like "stunsels", greatly increased the total sail area of a ship. These sails were set only in light or fair weather in an effort to catch the slightest breath of wind. Such a setting was used by Constitution when she was becalmed in the middle of a superior British force. So slight was the wind that the crew had to take to the ship's boats and pull Constitution ahead of her pursuers.

JCR

and done, her final bill was $302,718.84 – in modern terms, a cost over-run of some 260 percent. Quite predictably, Congress had called for an inquiry into the matter even before any of the "original three" had gotten to sea.[2]

One of Secretary of War McHenry's last tasks before turning over the Navy reins to Benjamin Stoddert had been to respond to this inquiry. He ascribed the "extraordinary expenditures" to five causes: (1) the building of the ships in different places, (2) the size of the ships, (3) the quantity of live oak used in their construction, (4) the rise in the price of materials and labor, and (5) certain losses and contingencies.

He straightforwardly admitted that "had it been determined to build the ships in one place, and in succession, instead of each in a different place, and all at the same time, it is certain that a considerable savings would have thereby accrued to the public." But, he noted, the law passed by the Congress had required that the ships be ready for operations "with little delay as possible." As it was doubtful that any one city was capable of accomplishing the task, it was decided to allocate construction to widely separated sites whose local economies could support the effort. Finally, in a particularly relevant barb to the politicians, the wealth was spread in this way to a half-dozen constituencies.

The upgrading of the characteristics of the ships from normally armed frigates of standard construction to heavily armed, heavily built "super frigates" was another cause of price rise. Not only were the characteristics changed, said McHenry, but the decision was made to use large quantities of live oak in lieu of white oak. Growing in a tidewater regime, live oak had been infinitely more difficult to procure. This, in turn, was exacerbated by the fact that not all timbers cut for shipment proved to be usable.

The rising costs of labor and materials has a modern ring to it. The Secretary reported that "the rise of wages alone, between the date of the first estimate and the time the frigates were launched, taking Philadelphia for the example, was from nine shillings to fifteen shillings per day; the rise in wrought iron and hemp, about forty percent; and on freight, one hundred percent."

Under the heading of "certain losses and contingencies" in McHenry's report, those which appear to have applied to *Constitution* include the loss of about fifty tons of hemp in a Boston fire, the interyard transfer of materials in 1796 when the program was cut back, and finally, the fact that timbers shipped generally were of a larger dimension than needed, upping the freight charges and increasing the work needed to fit them into the ship.

The Secretary informed Congress that he considered it "unfair" to have *Constitution*, *Constellation*, and *United States* bear the full onus of the inflated cost. The account included expenses incurred in efforts aborted in the years since 1794, such as those relating to the expected establishment of shipyards, in the safeguarding of assembled materials, and in the commencement, stoppage, and dismemberment of three hulls. These costs, he wrote, should be considered as peculiar to the day and not to be expected whenever a ship was built.

In concluding his report, McHenry observed that "after wisdom" is always better, and offered a thought for the future:

> "The great delay that has occurred in the present undertaking must always be more or less experienced, when heavy ships of war are required to be suddenly built, and the Government not previously possessed of the necessary timber and materials. It is certainly an unfit time to look for these, and prepare a navy yard, when the ships are required for actual service..."

Pregnant words which have not always been heeded.

NOTES

1. In addition to these weapons, the ship is known to have carried a number of swivels, possibly as many as twelve, sometimes mistakenly referred to as "howitzers" or "cannonades," with three-inch bores.

2. While comparisons of dollar-values in the 1790s and today are of questionable validity, it appears that, when related to the gross national products then and now, *Constitution*'s cost equates with that of a nuclear aircraft carrier.

Afterword

"Steady Breezes fine & Pleasant Weather.
"At 8 P.M. Took my departure from Boston Light House bearing W 1/2 N 3 1/2 Leagues dist."

So reads the first entry in the log of *USS Constitution*, a record that continues to be kept to this day. Since then, she has seen front-line service in three wars and been the vehicle in which some of the greatest of our naval heroes realized their moments of glory. As one of them, Commodore William Bainbridge, once said, "To have commanded the *Constitution* is a signal honor: to have been one of her crew, in no matter how humble a capacity, is an equal one." In the succeeding two centuries, the nation has seen fit repeatedly to name ships of the Navy in honor of their achievements and biographers to record their lives.

On the other hand, there are very few today who would recognize the name of Joshua Humphreys or could tell you what he contributed to the country. It was his design philosophy and creativity, however, that enabled *Constitution* thrice to defeat her adversaries in the War of 1812 and three times to escape from superior British forces. One would be hard pressed to have clearer confirmation of one's ideas than that. Without his genius, we would be without this legendary ship today. So let this small volume stand as a mark of respect honoring our first Naval Constructor, one of those far-sighted and dedicated men with which this nation was so blessed in its early years.

APPENDIX A

TABLE OF DIMENSIONS
A FRIGATE OF FORTY-FOUR GUNS

	Feet	*Inches*
Length of the gun deck, from the rabbet of the stem to post	174	10 1/2
Length of the keel for tonnage, allowing three-fifths of beam from twelve inches before the rabbet of the stem at the breadth line from the point where the three-fifths strike on the keel, to the rabbet on the post	145	
Moulded breadth of beam in the extreme part of the ship, which is at the upper edge of the second wale, and three and a half feet before the thirds of the keel, or one hundred feet two inches before the rabbet of the post	43	6
Height of the wing transom, above the rabbet of the keel	25	8 1/2
Height of the lower deck transom, above the rabbet of the keel	20	9
Top sides tumbles home amidships, at the under part of midship plank-sheer, or covering board	3	
Height of the lower deck, in the side above the rabbet, at	16	11
Plank on lower deck beams		3 1/2
Height between gun and lower deck	6	4
Gun deck plank		4
Height between decks, from gun to upper deck	7	
Upper deck plank		3
Waist amidship		3
Plank-sheer or covering board		4 1/2
To top of plank sheer	31	9

Height amidships of lower edge of the wale	17	11
Six strakes of wales, ten inches wide are	5	
Height from the top of the wale to port sill	3	3 1/2
Height of the port	2	11
Height from the top of the port to the top of the plank-sheer		4 1/2
Height from top of rabbet to top of plank-sheer is	31	9
Depth in the hold, taken from the strake next the limber strake	14	3
Height of the port sills on the quarter-deck and forecastle	1	10
Height on the gun deck	2	4
Height fore and aft	3	5
Height up and down	2	11
Ports - Distance between ports	7	5
After port, aft side, before the rabbet of the post	6	4
Fifteen ports on each side, besides the bridle or bow ports, if any		
Height of gun deck on the post, from a square line above the rabbet of the keel	27	
Height of gun deck on the stem, from a square line above the rabbet of the keel	24	10
Dead raising at two-fifths of the beam, for the breadth of the floor	2	9
Room and space	2	2

Height of the breadth line -
   amidships,   This line is the upper edge
   on the stem,   of the second wale, from
   on the transom, below all fore and aft.

Drifts - Quarterdeck and forecastle drifts, fourteen inches wide and three and a half inches thick.
Flush drift, twelve inches wide and four inches thick.
String, or first molding strake above the ports, fourteen inches wide, and four and a half inches thick.

Keel - Of good sound white oak, in three pieces; the middle piece to be not less than eighty feet, if to be had; scarfs not less than twelve feet, to be kept clear of the main and fore steps; sided in the midships eighteen inches; at the stem and post seventeen inches, and as deep as can be had; the scarfs all to be tabled and bolted with five bolts, one and one-eighth inches diameter; false keel six inches thick, but not to be put on until after the floor and keelson bolts are drove and riveted.

Keelson - Sided eighteen inches amidships, and sixteen inches fore and after end, and sixteen inches deep; scarfs not within fifteen feet of keel-scarfs, or main or fore-mast steps; upper keelson eighteen by fifteen inches deep, to be hooped and joggled into the lower one, all bolted with one and three-eighth inch bolts through every timber, and one in every cross-chock of one and one-eighth inches diameter.

Stem - In two pieces, if to be had; the lower one of good white oak, sided seventeen inches, and moulded not less than twelve inches clear of the rabbet; scarfs not less than four feet, to be tabled and bolted with three bolts, one and one-eighth inches in diameter.

Apron - Sided from twenty-eight to thirty inches at the upper end; and as the piece will work below, moulded at the upper end fourteen inches, and at the lower end seventeen inches.

Stern post - Eighteen inches square at the head, sided seventeen inches below by three and a half feet fore and aft, including false post, and ten inches thick on the aft side, at the keel, to be fitted for a crooked headed rudder.

Inner post - To be twelve inches, fore and aft, to run from the transom to the keel; to be of live oak, sided at head from twenty to twenty-four inches, and at the heel twelve inches.

Night-heads [sic] - Sided from sixteen to eighteen inches; moulded twelve inches at head, and fourteen below.

Hawse-pieces - To be four in number; sided eighteen inches, and to be bolted with one and one-eighth inch bolts into each other; their heels, if possible, to run down below the lower deck breast-hook.

Bow-timbers - Sided twelve inches, and as long as possible; their heels well secured into the dead-wood; to be in number on each side as per draught.

Hawse-holes - Two on each side; fifteen inches diameter, and fourteen inches on a square between each other.

Wing transom - Twenty-nine feet long on the aft side; moulded and sided twenty-two inches to round up, and aft six inches; all the others sided fourteen inches; the lower deck transom moulded as broad as can conveniently be had, for the better securing the ends of the deck plank; two bolts of one and one-eighth inches diameter in the deck transom and all above it; all below, bolted with one bolt of one and one-quarter inches diameter.

Fashion-pieces - Two pair, sided twelve inches and moulded fifteen inches on the cant, as hereafter directed.

Dead-wood, forward - To secure the scarf of the stem and keel together, sided the same as the apron at the heel; at the after end twenty-four inches, and not less than twenty inches moulded over the scarf of the keel, and to run sufficiently aft; midship dead-wood fourteen inches broad and nine inches thick, to run from the dead-wood forward to the stern-post knee, well fayed on the keel.

Rabbet of the main keel - To be cut one inch below the upper edge; the garboard strakes to fay well to the dead-wood all fore and aft; the dead-wood to be tarred and papered with good, thick, substantial tarred sheathing paper, in order to prevent the ship from sinking if she should lose her keel.

Stern post knees - Two good ones; the lower one as long as possible.

Floor and raising timbers - Of good white oak, sided twelve and a half inches; moulded at the floor sirmark fifteen inches, and in the throat, from the top of the dead-wood, twenty-one inches; to be bolted through the keel with one and three-eighths inch bolts; these bolts should be put as near the side of the keel as possible, in order to give room on the other side for the keelson bolts; one floor bolted near the larboard side of the keel, the other on the starboard side; the timber all to be double bolted from the foremast to within ten feet of the mizzenmast.

Lower futtocks - Of live oak, sided twelve inches in the midships, and something smaller at the fore and after ends of the ship, to butt against the side of the dead-wood amidships; to have crosschocks fayed on the dead-wood, and their heels to be bolted through the keelson and keel with one and one-eighth inch bolts.

Middle and upper futtocks and top timbers - Sided eleven and a half inches; top-timbers moulded at the gunwale seven inches; at the port sill nine inches; all the other timbers sized by a diminishing line from the port sill to the floor sirmark.

Timbers, framed - Floor timbers, lower futtocks, middle and upper, and top timbers, all to be framed in forms, and bolted with three bolts one and one-eighth inches square in each scarph, except the lower futtocks and floors, which should have one and one-fourth inch bolts. These timbers must be faced fair and true: for if they are out of winding, it will be impossible to level the timbers with any truth.

Main wales - six strakes on each side, seven inches thick and ten inches wide.

Black strakes, five in number - The first and second five and one-half inches thick; the third, five and one-fourth inches; the fourth, five inches; and the fifth, four and one-half inches thick, by ten inches wide; the upper edge of the black strake to be mitred down to a level, in order to carry the water out of the seam; plank between the black strake and the string, to be three and one-half inches thick.

Thick work under the wales - first strake six inches thick; and second, five and one-half inches; third, of five inches; and fourth, of four and one-half inches; run-king plank, in the bottom, four inches thick; to be not less than six feet scarf, nor less than four strakes between every two butts on the same timber; the seams all to be made a little out-gauged, and great care must be taken to bevel both edges of the plank that comes together alike: for, if one edge is hewn standing, the other must be under, which makes bad work, the plank with the under bevelling will caulk off.

Bilge strakes outside - one, of six inches thick; two, of five and one-half ditto; two, of four and one-half ditto, on each side, the middle strake to cover the butts of the timbers equally inside and out, to be reduced, fore and after ends, the same as the running plank.

Inside work - limber strakes - two on each side, six inches thick, and fourteen inches wide, to be bolted through the outside bilge strake, in every third timber, with one inch bolts.

Running ceiling plank - four inches thick.

Lower deck clamps - two strakes on each side, five inches thick, and one strake four and one-half inches, all hooked and joggled into each other, with hooks not less than two inches, reduced at fore and after ends.

Steps of masts - the fore step to be placed between two breast hooks; the main step to be left so as to be set either forward or aft, as occasion may require; mizzen step to be two crotchets, the arms of which ought to be run up as high as possible.

Pillars or stanchions - three tiers under the gun deck, and one under the upper deck, made to shift.

Breast hooks - of live oak, five in the hold, including the deck hooks, from eighteen to twenty feet long, if to be had, and bolted in every timber with bolts of one and one-fourth inch in diameter, as well as through the stem; and two between decks, secured as above, the deck breast hooks moulded as broad as possible, in order to give good hold for the deck planks.

Transom riders - two on each side, under the lower deck, eighteen feet long, and sided twelve inches, bolted in every other timber with one and one-eighth inch bolts.

Diagonal riders - six pair on each side, in the three principal pieces, with two shorter ones to complete the pair, tabled and bolted together with six iron bolts one and one-fourth inch square in each scarf, and three in the short pieces to be bolted through the bottom plank, at every two feet, with one and one-eighth inch copper bolts, the two midship ones to butt against each other; the foremost of the two midship riders to be cut with a bird's mouth, and to fit under the eighth beam from forward; the after one of the midship ones to be cut and fixed in the same manner under the eighth beam from aft the other riders, to be the distance of two beams apart, and fitted in he same manner, to be kept the same distance aft and forward at heel, as they are at the head, to be tenoned and bolted into the keelson.

Lower deck beams - of the best heart pitch pine, sided sixteen inches, and moulded fourteen inches; the longest beam to spring six inches, and the rest by the same mould.

Lodging knees - sided ten inches, body to reach the next beam and arm, six feet hooked into the beam; to lay two inches below the upper edge of the beam for the water ways, and thick stuff to joggle down, to be bolted with seven bolts one and one-fourth inch diameter.

Dagger knees - sided eleven inches, body nine feet long, and arm seven feet, the arm hooked into the beam, and bolted with eight one and one-fourth inch diameter bolts.

Lower deck transom knees - sided twelve inches, body ten and one-half feet long, arm seven feet, and bolted with thirteen bolts one and one-fourth inch diameter.

Carlings - in three tier, six and nine inches, of white oak.

Ledges - five by six inches, two between each beam.

Mast carlings - for the main and foremast, ten by thirteen inches, to be kneed with four good knees; mizzen carling six by twelve inches, and kneed in the same manner; all of which pieces to be of live oak, and bolted with inch and seven-eighths bolts; gun deck carlings the same size, and secured in the same manner.

Spar beams - one of live oak on each side of the main hatch, tabled, kneed, and bolted, on the foreside of the beam, on the after part of the main hatch, twelve inches by fourteen; and for gun deck the same.

Solid waterways - of good long substantial white oak, worked with a feint [sic] hollow, rabbeted one and one-quarter inch above the deck, allowing two inches to be let down upon the beams; a good six inch oak strake joggled two inches into the edge of the waterway, and into and over the beams and ledges for the gun deck; a five and one-half inch strake for the lower deck, and a five inch strake for the upper deck, all joggled in the same way, and bolted through the side every four feet, and through every beam, with one and one-eighth inch bolts, upper deck with inch bolts.

Thick strakes on lower deck - two strakes of white oak plank, five and one-half inches thick, and not less than ten inches wide, bolted and joggled into each other, and over and into the beams and ledges two inches, running all fore and aft along side of the hatches; two other strakes on each side, fitted as above, midway between the water ways and hatch strakes, a long white oak knee to be fayed at the end of each pair, to be joggled over two beams, well bolted to the bow and stem with one and seven-eighth inch bolts; and two other white oak knees, to run from the mizzenmast to the stern post, joggled over and into each beam, to be let down on the beams sufficient for the ledges to frame into them; one other to reach from the stem to the foremast, worked in the same manner; the arm part of each knee to be well bolted through the stern and post with one and one-fourth inch bolts.

Lower deck plank - to be three and one-half inches thick, of the best heart pitch pine, clear of all defects whatever.

Orlop deck - to be laid six feet two inches below the upper part of the lower deck; beams of the best heart pitch pine, sided twelve inches, and moulded ten inches, laid with two inch common plank, kneed with one good live oak knee at each end, bolted with inch bolts; it will be best to put the clamps on the ceiling three inches thick.

Spirkettings - two strakes on each side on lower deck, five inches thick, hooked and joggled into each other, fitting in plank between the list and clamps four inches thick.

Gun deck clamps - two strakes on each side, five inches thick, and one of four and one-half inches, joggled into each other two inches.

Gun deck beams - one under each port, and one between, of the best heart pitch pine, as near as the hatchways and masts will admit, as per draught, sided eighteen inches, and moulded fifteen inches; all other beams to be laid directly over and under the same.

Standard knees - twelve on each side on the lower deck, one to be fayed over each beam, the diagonal riders come under, and the others placed amidships, sided thirteen inches, body to reach the upper edge of gun deck clamps, the arm six feet long, and bolted with eight bolts one and one-fourth inch diameter.

Gun deck lodging knees - Sided ten inches, body to reach the next beam, arm six feet long, bolted with seven bolts of one inch and a quarter diameter.

Hanging knees - Seven feet body and six feet arm, sided eleven inches, bolted with eight bolts one inch and a quarter diameter; the arms of all knees to be hooked and joggled into their respective beams.

Gun deck transom knees - Sided twelve inches, body twelve feet long, arm seven feet, bolted with twelve bolts one inch and a quarter diameter.

Carlings - In three tiers, six by nine inches, of white oak.

Ledges - Five by six inches, of white oak, two between each beam.

Plank - Four inches thick, six feet from the side, of the best white oak, clear of all sap and other defects whatever, the rest to be laid of the best heart pitch pine, clear of all sap and other defects whatever.

Spirketting - To reach the port sill, and five inches thick; all scarfs should be kept clear of the ports; sill butts well shifted.

Filling-in plank - Between the spirketing [sic] and clamps, three inches thick.

Wing transom knees - Sided thirteen inches, body fourteen feet long, and arm eight feet, bolted with fourteen bolts, one inch and a quarter diameter.

Thick strakes - On the gun deck two strakes white oak plank six inches thick, and not less than ten inches wide, bolted and joggled into each other, and over and into the beams and ledges two inches, running all fore and aft along side of the hatches. Two other strakes on each side fitted as above, midway between the water way and hatch strakes.

Upper Deck

Clamps - Two strakes on each side, four inches thick, hooked and joggled into each other.

Beams - Placed over the gun deck beams, sided thirteen and fourteen inches, and moulded, of the best heart pitch pine.

Quarter deck transom - Ten by ten, one knee at each end, sided eight inches, body and arm six feet, and bolted with eight bolts one inch diameter.

Lodging knees - Sided seven inches and a half, body to reach the next beam, arm five to four and a half, hooked and joggled into every beam, and bolted with seven bolts one inch diameter.

Hanging knees - Sided eight inches, body six feet and a half long, and arm five feet, bolted with eight bolts one inch diameter.

Carlings - Three tiers, except where the long coamings are five by eight inches, white oak.

Ledges - Four and a half by six, white oak, two between each beam.

Mast coamings - To be of good white oak as well as the hatch coamings; those of the main and foremast should be at least six inches clear of the mast all round, in order to give room for the mast to play, and more particularly for heaving down; the mizzen partners need not exceed three inches clear.

Plank for deck - Three inches thick, five feet of which must be laid with oak from the side, the rest of the best heart pitch pine plank.

Long coamings - Of heart pitch pine, ten by seventeen inches, to be kept wide enough apart to take down the boat and room alongside for the men to pass from the gun to the upper deck.

Stemson - Of live oak, sided seventeen inches, and moulded ten inches, to shift the scarfs of stem and apron o reach the upper deck breast hook.

Leaden scuppers - On each side of the gun deck, cut elliptical, four by six.

Seat transom - Across the stern, the height of the port sill to be joggled into the counter timbers, nine inches thick, and kneed at each end with one iron knee, to fay all along under the gallery door, and long enough to receive three bolts before it of one inch diameter, the thwartship arm four feet, to be bolted with three bolts, one inch diameter.

Counter timbers - Of live oak, sided at the lower part of the windows and heel eleven inches, at the upper end six inches, to be filled in from the lower part of the window to the wing transom with red cedar, except in the wake of the gun room ports.

Cable bits [sic] - Two pairs, of good strong white oak, twenty two inches square, and to taper below the lower deck beams to sixteen inches, cross pieces to be twenty-two inches fore and aft, and twenty inches deep, to have a standard knee against each bit, sided fourteen inches, to run forward over three beams, and scored down over each two inches, the arm to run to the opposite side of the cross piece.

Catheads - Sided twenty inches and moulded eighteen inches.

Treenails - For the bottom, of the best heart locust, to drive after a one inch and three eighths auger; for the wales and upper works, to drive after a one inch and a quarter auger; to be all planes to a moot, and not suffered to be overhauled afterwards.

Source: *American State Papers*, Vol. I, Paper No. 2. Washington, DC: Gales and Seaton, 1834.

Note: At Captain Thomas Truxtun's urging, Secretary of War Knox authorized white oak substituted for pitch pine in the deck beams. Of the three original frigates, only *United States* had pitch pine deck beams.

APPENDIX B
JOSHUA HUMPHREYS' MATERIAL ESTIMATE FOR A 44-GUN FRIGATE

1 piece for keel 80 feet long, 18 by 24 inches in the middle
2 pieces for keel 55 feet long, 1 of 18 by 30 inches, and 1 of 18 by 23
1 stern post knee "as long as can be had"
1 stern keelson rider, and one for stem
1 piece dead wood forward
1 piece dead wood 24 inches by 8, 100 feet, or 2 of 50 feet
1 lower piece stem and five pieces for keelson 310 feet, 18 inches square
80 floor raising timbers and crotches
2000 feet of 6 1/2 inch wales 9 inches wide running measure
200 feet of 5 inch wales 9 inches wide running measure
4200 feet of wale stuff 6 by 9 for decks[1]
2000 feet of 4 inch plank for gun deck[1]
4000 feet scantling for carlings 6 by 6 reduced measure
1000 feet scantling for carlings 6 by 9 reduced measure
1 deck stem and 1 deck sternpost knee to mizen and foremast
1400 feet of 5 inch plank 12 inches wide for clamps[1]
600 feet of 6 inch plank 10 inches wide for limber streaks running measure[1]
1000 feet of 5 inch plank 14 inches wide for inside bilge streaks running measure[1]
1500 feet of scantling for carlings for orlop deck
18000 feet of 4 inch plank for bottom and sealing [sic], 200 good white oak logs
1000 feet running measure of 5 inch plank 900 of 4 1/2 inch and 5000 feet of 3 inch[1]
10000 feet of 3 1/2 inch heart pine plank for lower deck[1]
7000 feet of 4 inch heart pine plank for gun deck[1]

8000 feet of 3 inch heart pine plank for quarterdeck and forecastle[1]
54 heart pitch pine beams for lower deck 14 by 16, 30 to 42 feet long
60 heart pitch pine beams for gun deck 15 by 18, 30 to 40 feet long
12 heart pitch pine beams for forecastle 10 by 11, and 12 by 13, 22 to 35 feet long
34 heart pitch pine beams for quarterdeck 10 by 11 and 13 by 14, 28 to 36 feet long
50 heart pitch pine orlop beams 10 by 12, 30 to 38 feet long
6000 feet Jersey pine two inch plank for orlop deck[1]
170 live oak lower futhooks[2]
174 live oak middle futhooks[2]
178 live oak upper futhooks[2]
150 live oak top timbers[2]
50 cedar top timbers[2]
200 cedar half timbers[2]
2 live oak knight heads
8 live oak hausepiece
12 live oak bow timbers
1 live oak upper piece and 1 piece apron
40 live oak stanchions
1 live oak sternpost 30 feet long, sided 17 inches
1 live oak transom 30 feet long, 22 inches square and 10 smaller ones
2 live oak corner counter timbers
6 live oak middle counter timbers
12 cedar half timbers
500 knees for lower and gun deck of live oak
130 knees for quarterdeck and forecastle of live oak
2 knees for transom standard live oak
8 knees for transom of live oak
8 live oak breasthooks from 18 to 20 feet long
6 pieces for partners for masts live oak
200 feet 1 1/2 inch copper bolts for breasthooks
1600 feet 1 3/8 inch copper bolts for floor, keelson dead wood, and sternpost knees
850 feet 1 1/8 inch copper bolts for stem, stern, keel scarfs, rudder and riders

1550 feet 1 1/8 inch for but [sic] and bilge bolts
7 pair composition dovetail plates
12000 feet of sheet copper for bottom
5000 feet cedar, 1 inch, and of half inch
30000 feet boards and scantling
50000 locust trunnells, 18 inch, 24 inch, and 30 inches long

NOTES:

1. All the plank to be as long as possible 60 or 70 feet if possible.

2. Those timbers are calculated for four tier, but it is doubtful whether they can be produced that length, if not add 340.

Source: *Naval Documents Related to the United States Wars with the Barbary Powers*, Volume I. Washington, DC: Government Printing Office, 1939. Pp. 73-4.

APPENDIX C

SPECIFICATIONS FOR *CONSTITUTION*'S ORIGINAL 24-POUNDER LONG GUNS

Overall length	8' 0.00"
Diameter of the caliber	5.83"
External diameter of the breech at the vent	1' 7.35"
At the extremity of the second reinforce before the trunnions	1' 4.12"
Behind and before the muzzle ring and at the extremity of the muzzle mouldings	1' 0.12"
At the extremity of the second reinforce, 2 inches before the trunnions	5.15"
Thickness of the metal, in the direction of the vent, and also from the rear of the caliber, and in the direction of the bore ring	6.66"
Behind and before the muzzle rings, and at the extremity of the muzzle mouldings	3.35"
Total weight	45 cwt

Note: *Specified thicknesses were considered the heaviest in the world at the time (1794).*

Each cannon was to be cast solid and then "bored with machinery."

Proofing required:

First proof: 13.5 pounds powder, 2 wads, 2 shot.
Second proof: 15.75 pounds powder, 2 wads, 2 shot.
Third proof: 18.5 pounds powder, 2 wads, 2 shot.

Source: *American State Papers*, Vol. I, Paper No. 12.

APPENDIX D

MEMORANDUM FRIGATE *CONSTITUTION* STANDING RIGGING 1797

	Inches	fathom
Fore Stay	16	15
Preventer Stay	10.5	15
Shrouds	10	215
Sheets	5	83
Takles [sic]	8	45
Top mast Shrouds	6	100
Standing back Stays	6.5	111
Shifting back Stays	5	55
Top mast Stays	9	25
Preventer Stay	7.5	25
Main Stay	17.5	23
Preventer Do	13	20
Collar for main Stay	12.5	10
Shrouds	10	234
Sheets	5	88
Tacks	8.5	45
Top mast Shrouds	6	110
Back Stays	6.5	125
Shiftg. back-Stays	5	62
Top mast Stay	9	26
Preventer Stay	7.5	26
Mizen [sic] Stay	9	16
Shrouds	7	115
Top Mast Shrouds	4	56
Top Mast Stay	5.5	7

Reverse side of memo bears the legend:
"Dimensions of Rigging for *Constitution* Frigate"

Source: James Sever Papers, Library of Congress.

BIBLIOGRAPHY

Abbreviations used herein:

CAPT:	Captain
CDR:	Commander
COL:	Colonel
DNA:	National Archives
GPO:	Government Printing Office
LCDR:	Lieutenant Commander
LT:	Lieutenant
MHS:	Massachusetts Historical Society
MIDN:	Midshipman
RADM:	Rear Admiral
USNR:	U. S. Naval Reserve

MANUSCRIPT SOURCES:

Bryant, William. Letter Copy Book. Private collection.

Letter, Furnace Hope to Timothy Pickering, 23 Nov 1795. John Carter Brown Library, Brown University.

Letters, James Byers to Paul Revere, 18 Jun and 23 Oct 1795. MHS.

Letter, Tench Coxe to fifteen iron masters, 26 May 1794. M74, DNA.

Letters, Tench Coxe to Henry Knox, 7 Jun and 30 Dec 1794. M74, DNA.

_____, Tench Coxe to Paul Revere, 16 Jun, 21 Jul, and 10 Nov 1794. M74, DNA.

Letter, Tench Coxe to Paul Revere, 5 Sept 1794. MHS.

Letters, Tench Coxe to Samuel Hughes, 16 Jun and 18 Aug 1794. M74, DNA.

Letter, Tench Coxe to Brown and Francis, 20 Jun 1794. M74, DNA.

_____, Tench Coxe to Alexander Hamilton, 25 Jun 1794. M74, DNA.

_____, Tench Coxe to twenty-six addressees, 30 Jun 1794. M74, DNA.

Letters, Tench Coxe to all Navy Agents, 5 Jul 1794 and 31 Dec 1794. M74, DNA.

Letter, Tench Coxe to Robert Coleman, 11 Jul 1794. M74, DNA.

_____, Tench Coxe to M. De Rancy, 22 Jul 1794. M74, DNA.

_____, Tench Coxe to Elijah Phelps, 21 Aug 1794. M74, DNA.

_____, Tench Coxe to John Chester, 25 Sep 1794. M74, DNA.

_____, Tench Coxe to Nathaniel Cushing, 25 Sep 1794. M74, DNA.

_____, Tench Coxe to John Blegge, 24 Dec 1794. M74, DNA.

_____, Tench Coxe to Gardiner and Oldden, 3 Feb 1795. M74, DNA.

_____, Nathaniel Cushing to SecNav, 19 Oct 1819. M124, DNA.

_____, William Doughty to Henry Knox, 8 Feb 1796. Henry Knox Papers, Pierpont Morgan Library.

_____, Franklin M. Garrett to Virginia Steele Wood, 23 Apr 1976 (misdated 1977). Private collection.

_____, Alexander Hamilton to Paul Revere, 23 Jul 1794. MHS.

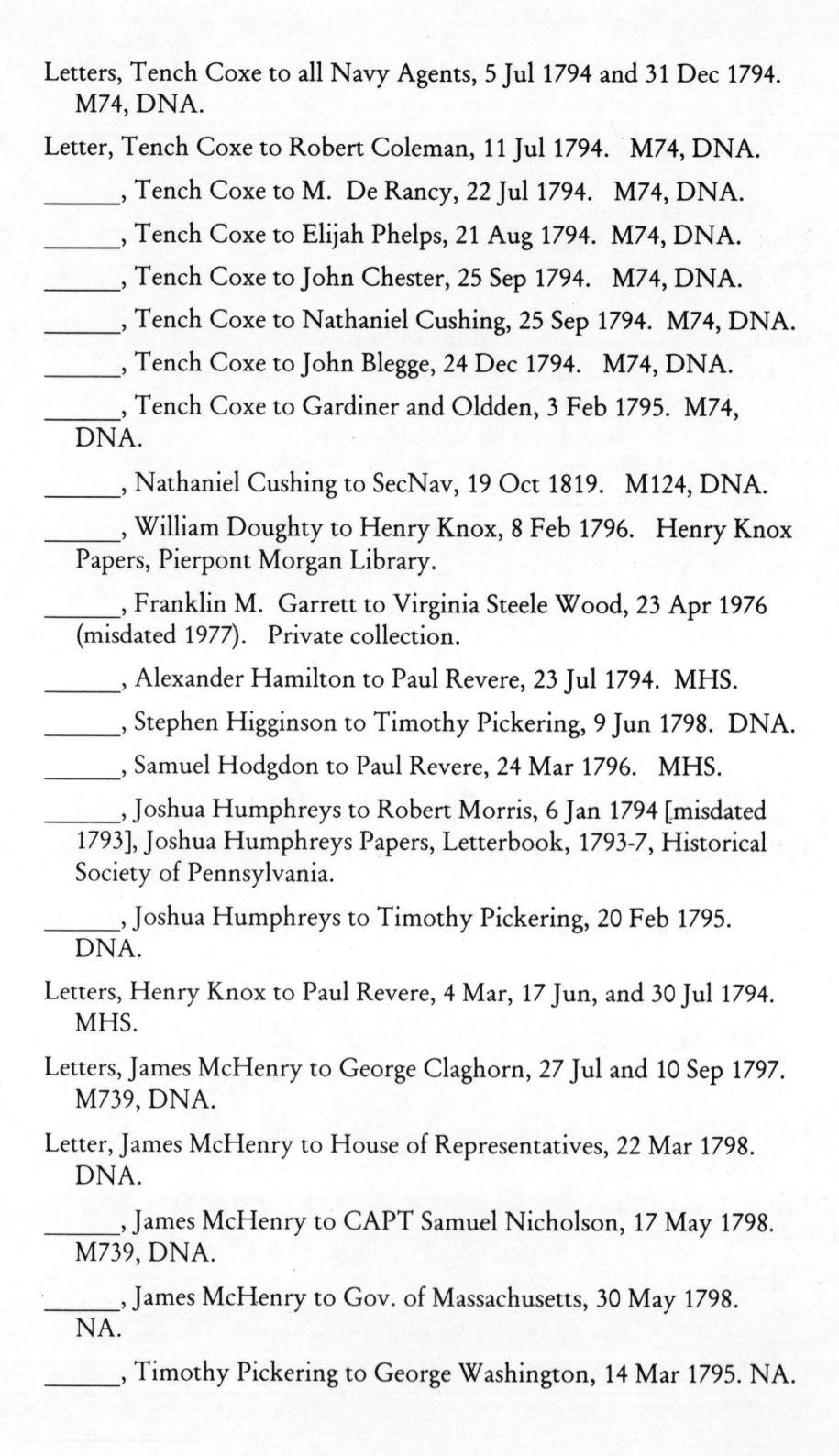

_____, Stephen Higginson to Timothy Pickering, 9 Jun 1798. DNA.

_____, Samuel Hodgdon to Paul Revere, 24 Mar 1796. MHS.

_____, Joshua Humphreys to Robert Morris, 6 Jan 1794 [misdated 1793], Joshua Humphreys Papers, Letterbook, 1793-7, Historical Society of Pennsylvania.

_____, Joshua Humphreys to Timothy Pickering, 20 Feb 1795. DNA.

Letters, Henry Knox to Paul Revere, 4 Mar, 17 Jun, and 30 Jul 1794. MHS.

Letters, James McHenry to George Claghorn, 27 Jul and 10 Sep 1797. M739, DNA.

Letter, James McHenry to House of Representatives, 22 Mar 1798. DNA.

_____, James McHenry to CAPT Samuel Nicholson, 17 May 1798. M739, DNA.

_____, James McHenry to Gov. of Massachusetts, 30 May 1798. NA.

_____, Timothy Pickering to George Washington, 14 Mar 1795. NA.

122

Letters, Timothy Pickering to Paul Revere, 3 Apr and 8 Sep 1795. MHS.

Letter, Quartermaster General of Massachusetts to the State General Court, 7 Feb 1800. MA State Library.

_____, Quartermaster General of Massachusetts to the Governor, 7 Jan 1805. MA State Library.

_____, Paul Revere to Tench Coxe, 31 Jul 1794. MHS.

_____, Paul Revere to Nelson Miller, 1 May 1795. MHS.

_____, Paul Revere to Henry Jackson, 28 Oct 1797. MHS.

_____, MIDN John Roche to his father, 19 Jun 1798. Robert Rogers Collection, William L. Clements Library, University of Michigan.

_____, COL Stephen Rochefontaine to Paul Revere, 22 Jun 1795. MHS.

PRINTED DOCUMENTS:

American State Papers, Vol. I. Papers 2, 3, 5-9, 12, 25, and 34. Washington: Gales and Seaton. 1834.

Navy Department. *Naval Documents Relating to the Quasi War with France*. Vol. I. Washington: GPO. 1935.

_____. *Naval Documents Relating to the Barbary Wars*. Vol. I. Washington: GPO. 1939.

MEMOIRS AND MONOGRAPHS:

Barrows, COL James S. *The Beginning and Launching of the United States Frigate Constitution*. A paper read before The Bostonian Society, 17 Feb 1925.

Brewington, Marion V. *Shipcarvers of North America*. New York: Dover Publications, Inc. 1962.

Cate, Margaret Davis. *Our Todays and Yesterdays*. Brunswick, GA: Glover Bros., Inc. 1930.

Chapelle, Howard I. *The History of the American Sailing Navy*. New York: Bonanza. 1949.

Chatterton, E. Keble. *Ship Ways of Other Days.* J. B. Lippincott Company. 1924.

Dodds, James, and Moore, James. *Building the Wooden Fighting Ship.* New York: Facts on File Publications. 1984.

Gorr, Louis F. "The Foxall-Columbia Foundry: An Early Defense Contractor in Georgetown." Reprint from *The Records of the Columbia Historical Society of Washington, D. C., 1971-72.* Washington: Columbia Historical Society. 1973.

Hazzard, William W. *St. Simon's Island, Georgia: Brunswick and Vicinity.* Virginia Steele Wood, ed. Belmont, MA: Oak Hill Press. 1974.

Hollis, Ira N. *The Frigate Constitution.* Boston: Houghton, Mifflin and Co. 1901.

Martin, CDR Tyrone G. *The Launch, or Huzzah for the Constitution.* Paper presented at the USS Constitution Museum, 16 Oct 1986.

Miller, Nathan. *Sea of Glory.* New York: David McKay Co. 1974.

Morison, Samuel Eliot. *The Oxford History of the American People.* New York: Oxford University Press. 1965.

Paullin, Charles Oscar. *Paullin's History of Naval Administration, 1775-1911.* Annapolis: U.S. Naval Institute. 1968.

Pinckney, Pauline A. *American Figureheads and Their Carvers.* New York: W. W. Norton & Co. 1940.

Records of the Columbia Historical Society of Washington, D. C., Vol. II. Washington: Columbia Historical Society. 1908.

Reilly, John C., Jr. *Ships of the U. S. Navy: Christening, Launching, and Commissioning.* Washington: GPO. 1975.

Rowe, William H. *The Maritime History of Maine.* New York: W. W. Norton & Co. n. d.

Smelser, Marshall. *The Congress Founds the Navy.* South Bend: University of Notre Dame Press. 1959.

Snow, RADM Elliot, and Gosnell, LCDR H. Allen. *On The Decks of 'Old Ironsides'.* New York: Macmillan Co. 1932.

Tucker, Glenn. *Dawn Like Thunder.* New York: Bobbs Merrill. 1963.

ARTICLES:

Ferguson, LT Eugene S. USNR. "The Launch of the United States Frigate Constellation." U. S. Naval Institute *Proceedings*, September 1947, pp. 1091-1095.

Martin, CDR Tyrone G. "Top Guns in the Early Sailing Navy." *Man at Arms*, Jul/Aug 1987, pp. 12-20.

_____. "Joshua Humphreys' Real Innovation." *Naval History*, Mar/Apr 1994, pp. 32-37.

Stanton, Elizabeth Brandon. "Builder of the First American Navy." *Journal of American History*, Vol. II, No. 1 (1908), pp. 101-112.

Valette, Henry M. "History and Reminiscences of the Philadelphia Navy Yard." *Potter's American Monthly Magazine*, Jan 1876.

UNPUBLISHED MATERIALS:

Martin, CDR Tyrone G. "A Most Fortunate Ship." Revised and expanded manuscript. 1996.